Hope in the Darkness

A Medical Professional's Guide to Gospel Centered Care

Sara Danielle Hill

For those who have poured out their hearts and souls caring for "the least of these"

Contents

Preface

This book was birthed out of my years of treating serious illnesses and witnessing the depravity in my patients' lives. Throughout most of my nursing career, I have been passive, the opposite of great figures like Dietrich Bonhoeffer, Corrie Ten Boom, and William Wilberforce. These individuals were people of action. They firmly believed in their principles, and their lives were defined by the actions they took.

For too many years I knew that Jesus was the answer to many of my patients' problems but felt no urgency or desire to put these beliefs into action. I felt a gnawing unease at my inability to help my patients through their hardships to the extent I wanted, but I pacified it. This manifested in ignoring the deep issues I was faced with. If I was really brave, I might occasionally pray with a patient in their room or share an inspirational quote with them. I genuinely hoped that this would soothe their aching heart. At that time, though, I still believed that my focus was medical, not spiritual. I still believed that medication was the main answer, and besides, I didn't have time to share the gospel anyway.

It was almost a decade into my career when I noticed myself becoming more and more dissatisfied with my approach to caring for patients. I attribute these feelings of restlessness to the working of the Holy Spirit in my life. I struggled in my attempt to help patients and their families navigate through their wreckage, much of which was caused by sin. With the surge in suicide, abuse, addiction, and human trafficking, I wondered how the Bible and Jesus fit into the picture. The deeper I journeyed into my nursing career, the more I felt myself floundering. I wrestled as my spiritual questions stacked higher and higher in the face of an ever-present darkness.

Gradually, the Lord has changed my perspective by challenging me to see my patients and their families as he does—as people lost and without hope, broken and in need of a Savior. It began with the thought,

"OK, I'm going to be more intentional about praying consistently for my patients." This grew into praying and looking for opportunities to have conversations that might point my patients to Christ.

This change in perspective then led me to question my unique role as a Christian who is a nurse. Recently, I recalled a small lesson on spirituality in nursing school. The argument was made that a patient's spiritual wellbeing is tied to their encompassing quality of life. The point of the lesson that stuck out to me was that if a nurse is going to care for the individual holistically, they must account for the patient's spiritual health or vitality. As I reflected on the lesson, it struck me that there was a gaping hole in my nursing practice, even by secular standards. If I truly believed that Jesus was the way, the truth, and the life, how would I bring him into my patient care? And how did he fit into brokenness?

To answer these questions, we are going to dive deep into the biblical truths of sin, illness and healing, spiritual warfare, and a Christ-centered perspective. I don't know about you, but I am tired of the incapable shallowness of self-help books, and I long for the deep richness of God's Word in life application.

There is a lot of mess that we will wade through. I hope that through it Christ will challenge your perspective, your heart, and your perceptions. I am so looking forward to wrestling through these issues with you, and I do not use the word *wrestle* lightly. Any time God is working to change our hearts and minds it can be difficult and painful. However, my prayer is that you will walk away from this conversation with a deeper understanding and love for your Creator and a renewed vigor to serve him.

Before we begin, I want to encourage you. You are here for a purpose. Healthcare is hard, and it is only getting more difficult, but the Lord has placed you in your specific position and location for a purpose. As we work through some hard topics together, I hope you will begin to ask to Lord what his plan is for you and how you can serve him best. The Lord is enough, dear friend. Lean into him.

Sin

I remember sitting at the front desk reviewing the day's patients with the nurse from the previous shift. The floor was full; it had clearly been an eventful night. My co-worker looked worn-out. Her eyes held the same heaviness that my heart felt. Eight suicide attempts on our unit in the past 12 hours, and there was an unpredictable autistic kid to think about as well. I rubbed my hand across my forehead. It was going to be a long and crazy shift. I could feel it.

Sadly, this had become the new norm. Many people in the hospital I worked at marveled at the compassion we exuded as a unit and formed a consensus to add medical psychiatry to our specialty mix of patients. Now, not only were we dealing with helping families through hard, chronic diagnoses, we were riding the emotional roller coaster of the psychiatric world. What had set us apart as a unit? At least half of the nurses were professing Christians. Christ was shining through, and people were noticing. However, after a year of riding through this unknown territory, the strain was evident. People were leaving, burnout was eminent, our vigor had been sapped away.

As I read through the patients' charts that day, my heart broke over and over. These kids, and sometimes their families, were living through hell. This was the exact example of devastation that sin leaves in its wake. Never in my life had I looked evil in the face and had it stare so blatantly back at me. My world was rocked. *Jesus, where are you?!* my heart cried as I combed through a particularly horrific case. How could I reconcile truths and characteristics I knew to be true about God (e.g. he is good, just, loving, and merciful) with the carnage I saw on a daily basis? Where was God in the midst of this wreckage? And how could I even begin to scratch the surface of helping my patients through their brokenness? Also, if I believed that the Bible was true, without error, and applicable to all aspects of life, then where and how were these situations addressed in the Bible?

Sometimes the Lord slowly draws you into a hard spot of growth. However, in this season the Lord grabbed me and pulled me into the deep end with him. I began to seek answers in the Bible out of desperation. As I looked at my patients' lives and the incredible hardships they were going through, I kept coming back to sin. I am not saying that they were sick because of sin, though in some circumstances that may be the case, I am saying that the rampant sin in the world was at the root of the issue. I know what you are thinking! All your warning flags are going up. Please, bear with me, as I will, over this chapter, endeavor to explain.

Defining Sin

The Bible shows us exactly why our world is so screwed up, and I would like to unpack it with you. Let's go back to the beginning. Why do we turn on the news or scroll through Facebook or Twitter and cringe? We know the world is not as it should be. It is evident through the brokenness in people's lives. As believers, we know that is because of sin. So, let's talk about sin.

It is important to begin this discussion by first addressing sin, because we will never understand the brokenness, depravity, and hopelessness our patients feel unless we have a clear understanding of sin. In the same way sin has knitted itself into the fabric of humanity, it has also woven itself into every aspect of life on earth. Merriam-Webster defines sin as "a transgression of divine law; any act regarded as such a transgression, especially a willful or deliberate violation; any reprehensible or regrettable action."[1] It is probably safe to say that if the majority of humanity were polled, they would agree with this definition. Globally, we see sin strictly an action or series of actions. This, however, is not what God's Word teaches. The Bible teaches over and over that there is more to sin than the actions performed.

To comprehend what is happening today, we need to start at the beginning, when sin first entered the world. At the end of Genesis 1, we see the world newly created and functioning as God intended. Everything was "very good" in the sight of God. Then God created Adam, gave him a mate, Eve, and placed them in a beautiful garden in the midst of perfect creation. Then God commanded them, "You may surely eat of every tree in the garden, but of the tree of the knowledge of good and evil you shall not eat, for in the day that you eat of it you shall surely die" (vv. 16–17). Seems easy right? Well, keep on reading. In the next chapter everything changes, and not for the best. The serpent comes to Eve and tempts her to disobey God. She listens to him and decides that she will indeed disobey God. She even convinces her husband, Adam, to do so as well. Suddenly, everything was altered. Their eyes were opened; they realized they were naked and tried to cover their nakedness.

OK, let's pause and consider, what was the sin? Was it the act of eating the fruit? Was it the willful disobedience of God's command? Was it the desire to be like God, exhibited in Adam and Eve's choice to make their own judgment call? Was it the decision to seek the betterment of themselves outside of God? Or the desire to find their own way? I would argue yes. Yes to all. In action, Adam and Eve sinned by disobeying God, but in their hearts they sinned as well. Romans 1:25 says, "they exchanged the truth about God for a lie and worshiped and served the creature rather than the Creator, who is blessed forever!" Adam and Eve exchanged all that they knew about God (that he is good, loving, sufficient for all needs, and the source of all wisdom) for the lie that they could find satisfaction and fulfillment elsewhere. They made themselves to be more important than God by choosing their way over his. Therefore, the Bible teaches through this story that sin, by nature, is twofold. It is an action performed, deliberately and willfully, contrary to God's standards, *and* it is also a heart condition.

---

[1] "sin." *Merriam-Webster.com.* 2019. https://www.merriam-webster.com (18 Feb 2019).

There is still a little more to grasp about sin, so lets unpack Eve's actions in even more detail. I mentioned previously that Eve was no longer satisfied with God. We know this because she looked at the tree and saw "that the tree was to be desired to make one wise" (Genesis 3:6). Suddenly, as she was looking at this tree and listening to the serpent, she began to look outside of God for satisfaction, wisdom, and provision. The Apostle James speaks to this in his letter to the early church. He says, "But each person is tempted when he is lured and enticed by his own desire. Then desire when it has conceived gives birth to sin, and sin when it is fully grown brings forth death" (James 1:14–15). James is telling us that the action that we would name as sin is the outpouring of what is already at work in our heart. Let me say it another way. The heart is the root of the problem, and the action is the tell which reveals the state of the heart that is turned away from God. Pastor John Piper further elaborates on our understanding by saying, "Sinning is any feeling or thought or action that comes from a heart that does not treasure God above all other things."[2]

Let me illustrate this concept for you, because this bend that we all have is so insidious, deceptive, and subtle that often we are clueless of our wandering from God. If we pause, we can usually identify things we tend to treasure above him. Some of us might think of our love of things or the comfort we feel in a growing savings account. In my case, I unknowingly fostered this sinful bend in regard to my career. For years I looked at my long hours spent serving others; cleaning excrement; educating patients, families, and new nurses; and the prestige that comes with my hard-earned title as my fulfillment and the definition of who I was. As if my work would make me more satisfied and fill the restlessness of my soul. No, beloved. That. Is. Sin. It is only Christ Jesus who brings meaning and definition to the sweat and tears, the hours of service, and difficult patient care. I was never satisfied, nor could I ever have been because I was looking for satisfaction in the wrong place. For years I was foolish and blind, as was Eve the moment she began believing she could be satisfied and fulfilled anywhere else but with her Creator.

---

[2] John Piper, "What is Sin? The Essence and Root of All Sinning" (Desiring God, 2015).

Now that we have discussed the first sin in this world, let's delve a little deeper into the characteristics of sin. We know sin is an action, as described in Galatians 5:19–21, which says,

"Now the works of the flesh are evident: sexual immorality, impurity, sensuality, idolatry, sorcery, enmity, strife, jealousy, fits of anger, rivalries, dissensions, divisions, envy, drunkenness, orgies, and things like these. I warn you, as I warned you before, that those who do such things will not inherit the kingdom of God."

It's pretty obvious, right off the bat, that these actions described are wrong, even by the moral standards of most of our non-Christian peers. There is, however, a consequence to such overt sinful action, and Paul is very clear about God's stance on these activities. Anyone who does such things will have no part in God's kingdom.

Notice, Paul uses the word *inherit*. In order to inherit something, you must be in good standing with the person from whom you are inheriting, or else that individual might "write you out of the will," so to speak. They would disinherit you. Therefore, the implication of Paul using the word *inherit* is this: if you practice deeds that are contrary to God's standard, you will not be in his favor and you will miss out on all the good things he has in store for you. This is how our actions condemn us.

Now, let's connect sin to the inner motives and state of our hearts. In Romans 7:5, Paul talks about our sinful passions being at work in us to produce death. Even if there were no sinful actions performed, we are already characterized by sin because our passions give us away. In this same verse, Paul talks about "living in the flesh." This phrase refers to our sin nature. By nature, our hearts are characterized by sin. Our hearts are accustomed to it and comfortable in this state because it is a part of our daily life.

Let me give you a visual to work with. When thinking about how our sin nature reveals our true state, I get this image of a worm eating away at an apple from within. When the apple was formed it grew with the worm inside of it, and so bit by bit the apple is consumed. Just as the apple is diseased by the worm, so our hearts are sickened by sin. One day the worm will finish off the apple, and sin unchecked will eat us alive.

When you read through the Gospels, you repeatedly see that Jesus is frustrated with the Jews' obsession with actions and disregard for their diseased hearts. He gets on to the religious leaders in Matthew 23:23–24 for this very thing. In the Gospel of Mark, he addresses at length the heart of the individual and what truly corrupts a person. He says,

> "What comes out of a person is what defiles him. For from within, out of the heart of man, come evil thoughts, sexual immorality, theft, murder, adultery, coveting, wickedness, deceit, sensuality, envy, slander, pride, foolishness. All these evil things come from within, and they defile a person" (Mark 7:20–23).

Jesus shows us that sin is not only what you do; it is who you are on the inside that corrupts. In Genesis 6:5, Moses speaks to the issue plainly: "The LORD saw that the wickedness of man was great in the earth, and that every intention of the thoughts of his heart was only evil continually."

If sin is a state of the heart from which our actions are birthed, then it must be intrinsic to who we are. We briefly touched on this earlier when we mentioned "living in the flesh." We said earlier that when Paul was talking about "living in the flesh" he was talking about our sin nature. By definition, *nature* means "the inherent character of basic constitution of a person or thing; humankind's natural or original condition."[3] Therefore, by saying we have a sin nature, Paul is saying that our original, natural, or inherent condition is characterized by sin. It is who we are; it is innate. David understood this to be true. He sang about it in the Psalms. In Psalm 51:5, he says, "Behold, I was brought forth in iniquity, and in sin did my mother conceive me." Again in 58:3, he says, "The wicked are estranged from the womb; they go astray from birth, speaking lies." I like John Piper's simple and concise statement about sin. He says, "So you may rest forever the notion that your sin is

---

[3] "nature." *Merriam-Webster.com*. 2019. https://www.merriam-webster.com (20 Feb 2019).

mainly what you do or don't do. It is not mainly what you do. It is mainly who you are."[4]

Not only is it who I am or who you are, sin is who *we* are. Paul says in his letter to the Romans, "for *all* have sinned and fall short of the glory of God" (3:23, author's emphasis). He also says, "*None* is righteous, no, *not one*; *no one* understands; *no one* seeks for God. *All* have turned aside; together they have become worthless; *no one* does good, *not even one*" (vv. 10–12, author's emphasis). There is not one person on this planet, except for our Lord, Jesus Christ, who has ever been without sin. He alone is the exception to the rule.

Let me pause here. Take a deep breath. I know this is weighty. I realize I am throwing A LOT of scripture at you, but if the Bible has so much to say about sin, it is something important that we must take seriously. We must fully understand sin in order to develop the appropriate urgency to pull our patients from its jaws of death.

The Cost of Sin

The song "Eat You Alive" by The Oh Hellos runs through my mind every time I think about how deadly sin is. As a kid I never liked it when authors would include the lyrics to a song in a book. J. R. Tolkien was notorious for putting lyrics in the middle of a story. I always jumped over the songs, but I hope you will read these lyrics. They paint such a grotesquely perfect picture of sin:

> *He said to me,*
> *Child, I'm afraid for your soul*
> *These things that you're after, they can't be controlled*
> *This beast that you're after will eat you alive*
> *And spit out your bones.*
>
> *She'll string you along and she'll sell you a lie,*
> *But there's nothing but pain on the edge of a knife,*
> *There's no courage in flirting with fear*
> *To prove you're alive.*
>
> *I've seen the true face of the things you call life,*

---

[4] Piper, John. "What is Sin? The Essence and Root of All Sinning." *Desiring God.* 2015.

The voice of the siren that hold your desires,
But death, she is cunning, and cleaver as hell
And she'll eat you alive.[5]

Paul addresses the seriousness of sin in Romans. He says, "For the wages of sin is death" (6:23). A wage is a payment given in exchange for work. So, the payment we are due in return for sin is death. Later in the same book Paul stresses that life in our natural state, in our flesh, always and only results in death (7: 13-23). Furthermore, in his letter to the Ephesian church, he says, "And you were dead in the trespasses and sins." Therefore, we are, in our natural state, apart from God, clothed in death, and there is no hope, no cure.

I hope you feel the heaviness I feel. This is how I once was—hopelessly doomed in my sin, shrouded in death. It was inescapable. Brother and sister, *this is who you once were.* Remember the hopelessness from which you were plucked. Feel the weight. And this is still the state of the vast majority of your patients and peers.

Sadly, the bad news does not stop there! Not only are we dead and without hope, the consequence of a life lived apart from Christ is eternal punishment. Jesus warns that those who do not follow him will "go away into eternal punishment" (Matthew 25:46). Paul warns the Thessalonian church, in his second letter to them, that in the end, those who do not know God and have rejected his good news of salvation will "suffer the punishment of eternal destruction, away from the presence of the Lord and from the glory of his might" (1:8–10).

Let's pause and allow this reality to sink in. Your patients who do not know Christ are not only hopeless and headed for certain death, they are facing an ETERNITY of hopelessness because of their sinful nature. This is the chasm from which you were saved, friend. This is the chasm from which we must work to save our patients.

Everything in me wants to power through and get to the good stuff—the saving grace of Jesus Christ! However, let me just recap what we have discussed, because we covered a lot of ground, and it's tough terrain! Stay with me as we chew a bit longer on this meaty topic so we can fully digest what God is showing us.

We are stained by sin. However, unlike a bloodstain, no amount of club soda or oxy-clean can fix this problem. Like someone with

---

[5] The Oh Hellos, "Eat You Alive," *Through the Deep, Dark Valley* (2012).

vitiligo, sin who we are, down to our genetic makeup. Our hearts are overflowing with it, our minds are filled with it, and our actions give us away.

We are driven by instinct to rebel against God. The apostle John describes humanity as a people who love darkness instead of the light because their works, our works, are evil (John 3:19). "For the mind that is set on the flesh is hostile to God, for it does not submit to God's law; indeed, it cannot," Romans 8:7 says. Our sinful, rebellious hearts separate us from God. We are dead, we reek of evil, and we are without hope, apart from Christ.

Chew on this today. This thick hunk of meat that is hard to swallow and slow to digest. Let the heaviness of this chapter sit on your heart. I want to encourage you to take time to pray for the people in your life who do not follow Jesus. Beg the Lord to save them. They are dead without him. ONLY in Jesus is there hope, life, and salvation! Jesus said in John 14:6, "I am the way, and the truth, and the life. No one comes to the Father except through me."

2

This Broken World

When I was nine years old, my family packed all that we owned into ten footlockers and five carry-ons, boarded a plane, and made the three-day trip to Indonesia. After years of preparation for a calling to missions, my parents had finally taken the leap of faith. They flew away from everything they had ever known—all certainty, known comforts, family and friends—and moved their three young children to the largest Muslim country in the world.

There is nowhere in the world quite like that beautiful, sticky, chaotic land that I call home. The air is always warm, thick with humidity, and heavy with smells. Even now, I can almost taste the diesel-tinged, sewer-tainted, spicy mix of scents. For the average American, the onslaught of smells and the striking uniqueness of tropical life are often overwhelming, but to me they are sweet. Indonesia is a land of beauty—lush jungles, pristine beaches, vibrant coral, dramatic mountain ranges, and scenic vistas.

When an Indonesian talks about their country, they refer to it as their *air tanahku*. This means, literally, "my water land." What a perfect descriptor for that vast archipelago! I do not have enough words to describe the beauty of the land and ocean, the warmth of the people, or the robust culture. Indonesia is unlike any other place in the world. It gets under your skin and dives into your heart. Before you know what has happened, you're in love and will always be so.

Contrary to popular belief, the great majority of missionaries do not live in the jungle (though there are plenty who do). My parents served Christ in the overcrowded metropolis of Jakarta, the nation's capital. This teeming anthill of a city is alive with the blending of the East and West. All of the nation's 300 ethnicities are represented, and a large and growing international community contributes to the young nation's economy.

When I was in middle school, my family moved to the west side of the city. It was crowded, prone to flood in the rainy season, and home to one of the city's red light districts. It was here, under a dirty overpass, that we met Mega. Mega was a sweet little girl of about seven or eight. She was one of the millions of "street children" that filled the already overcrowded capital, but she had so much life in her eyes. We quickly formed a relationship with her. Every day we would see her at her usual spot at the stoplight, begging for money and playing with the other kids. She would see our car and come running over with a gaggle of children behind her. They were all so impressed that she knew not just one foreigner but a whole family! At the light we would chat. My parents would warn her to be careful in the traffic and give her some money or food, and then we would be off on our way. This was our habit for years.

My freshman year of high school, I moved off to boarding school, about ten hours away. I remember my mom calling me one day and asking me to pray for Mega because they had not seen her for a few days at the light and were worried about her. I came home a short time later on break and found out that Mega had reappeared about a couple of weeks after her disappearance. I will never forget the look of deep sorrow and anger on my dad's face when he told me that the last time he had seen her she was high. She had apparently taken to huffing glue. We saw her once at the light during my week of vacation. She reluctantly came over to our car. Her eyes haunt me to this day—empty, glassy, hopeless. My dad drilled her about where she had been and what she had been doing. Her father had been selling her. She made more money when she was sold for sex. She hated him, but there was no escape. I never saw her again after that conversation. She was only eleven or twelve.

Even now I weep as I think of her. Her story is not uncommon. In fact, I bet there are millions of girls with similar stories. Mega was my first real, tangible experience that taught me that the world is very broken. I mean, I had seen poverty and sickness, but I had never before seen the progression of the devastation that this evil world creates. As healthcare providers, we know (more than most) how incredibly sick and evil our world is.

The Inescapable Power of Sin

In the last chapter we discussed what sin is on an individual level, but I would now like to show you what the Bible says about sin on a global level, the power that sin has, and the hope we have in Christ Jesus! We've looked at Genesis 3 and discussed sin's entrance into the world.

Turning over to Genesis 4, we get a picture of how profoundly sin affects mankind. This chapter is the classic Sunday school story of Cain and Abel. I'm sure most of us remember the story, but I would like to dig in deeper to uncover what is going on below the surface. I think you will find there is much more to this story than the lesson that murder is wrong. In fact, I would say that this story of two brothers is a warning. It warns the reader of having an attitude and heart like Cain and of the power of sin in the life of the individual, and ultimately society.

Recall that Genesis 4:3–5 tells of a time when Cain and Abel brought their offerings to the Lord. Cain brought fruits of the ground, and Abel brought a sacrifice from his flock. There is very little description of Cain's offering, implying that it was unremarkable. Abel, though, not only brought the best that he had, "the firstborn of his flock" (v. 4), but also went above and beyond, bringing "their fat portions." Notice God's reaction to each offering, "And the LORD had regard for Abel and his offering, but for Cain and his offering he had no regard" (vv. 4-5).

The difference between the two offerings that evoked God's displeasure with Cain was not that Cain offered grain while Abel offered an animal. Rather, it was that Cain brought the bare minimum and Abel brought an abundance. As one commentator put it, "Abel went out of his way to please God, whereas Cain was simply discharging a duty."[1]

---

[1] Walter L. Baker, et al., *The Bible Knowledge Commentary: Old Testament*, ed. John F. Walvoord (Colorado Springs: Cook Communications Minitries, 1983) 34.

Hebrews 11:4 explains that Abel's desire to please God was rooted in his faith, and his faith-rooted desire to please God was exemplified in his abundant offering. Because of the right state of his heart, God considered him righteous and was pleased with him. Cain, on the other hand, begrudgingly obeyed. And his wickedness and hard heart did not end there. Throughout the rest of Genesis 4 we see his rebellious nature unfold. In verses 6–7, God says, "Why are you angry, and why has your face fallen? If you do well, will you not be accepted?" In other words, God is saying, "Do what is right, seek me, and you will have the acceptance you desire." God used the prophet Hosea to say the same thing to the Israelites: "For I desire steadfast love and not sacrifice, the knowledge of God rather than burnt offerings" (Hosea 6:6).

This story of two brothers still speaks to the state of the human heart today. Cain and Abel represent two kinds of people on this earth: those who want to please God and those who don't but still want God to accept them anyway. The latter was Cain. He did not really cherish or want to follow God. He did not find pleasure and joy in obeying God, nor did he really want to do what was right by God's standards (as was shown in his sacrifice), but he still expected the same acceptance from God that Abel received. I mean, stop and think about that! What a twisted way of thinking! We are not just talking about a rebellious heart but a heart that is hard toward God.

Let me paint you a picture of where Cain's heart and head were. Cain was like a teenager who for Mother's Day gets a crayon and haphazardly scribbles a little card to his mom. Very little effort is put into this card. It is a last-minute solution to a day forgotten or unimportant to him. His sibling, in comparison, has outdone himself by getting his mother flowers, chocolates, and a necklace. In fact, to get his mother such a lavish gift, he used his entire month's paycheck that could have gone toward paying for college. The first brother expects his mother to be equally pleased with his half-hearted, poorly executed attempt at a card as she is with his bother's gift. Of course, though the mom loves both of her sons, she would be disappointed in her first son's gift and overjoyed with the second son's gift. This is how Cain and Abel respectively approached God.

In verse 6 of Genesis 4, we see God give Cain a reality check, and in verse 7 a warning. The second part of verse 7 is key. It says, "And if you do not do well, sin is crouching at the door. Its desire is contrary to you, but you must rule over it." I love Timothy Keller's paraphrase of this statement: "You do not know the power of sin in your heart. You underestimate sin."[2] In these two verses God is checking Cain in his hardness and rebelliousness and warning him of the power of sin in his heart. Verse 8 proves God to be right, for it's in this verse that Cain kills his brother, Abel.

To this point in the chapter we have seen a rebellious root in Cain bloom into hard-heartedness and murder. For the rest of the chapter we see this rebellion against God play out over and over. When confronted with the sin of murder in verse 9, Cain's unrepentant and callous response is, "I do not know; am I my brother's keeper?" When God punishes Cain, he rebels and complains, shirking the responsibility for his actions. He even defies God's curse of wandering by choosing to settle in the city of Nod.[3] This is why Cain is considered evil. Not just because he committed murder, but also because his heart was always rebellious and unrepentant, just like the devil's.[4]

Finally, in verses 17–24 we learn that this rebelliousness was passed down and taught to Cain's descendants. One descendant altered God's plan for marriage by marrying two women. This same man committed murder and, like his forefather, shirked responsibility for his actions. Though Cain and his family flourish, they are, as a whole, godless. Their godlessness is exhibited in their lifestyle, consumed by the pursuit of pleasure and of self.[5] We have seen this play out before, in the first created humans. This chapter is showing us that sin has multiplied through the generations, and we now begin to see it play out on a global scale. This is how our vast world is filled with rebellious people, and, sadly, the majority of people have "walked in the way of Cain" (Jude 10–11).

In Romans 1:18–32, Paul addresses in detail the decline of mankind and the progression of a rebellious heart into depravity. In verses 18–19 he says that the knowledge of God (who he is, his character, his attributes) is repulsive to those who rebel against God, so much so that they suppress the truth about God. Though these attributes of God "have been clearly perceived, ever since the creation of the world" (Romans 1:20), a rebellious heart will always try to blind itself

---

[2] Keller, Timothy, "Sin as Predator," *Gospel In Life* (1996).

[3] Walter L. Baker, et al., The Bible Knowledge Commentary: Old Testament (1983) 34.

[4] 1 John 3:12

[5] Walter L. Baker, et al., The Bible Knowledge Commentary: Old Testament (1983) 35.

and others from the obvious truth about God. In verses 20–21, Paul names the root of suppressing the knowledge of God as the desire to avoid glorifying and thanking him. In essence, the rebellious individual is trying to remove God from his rightful place of authority and preeminence.

This is where the decline begins. From the end of verse 21 through verse 22 we see that rebellion against God is not without a cost: "but they became futile in their thinking, and their foolish hearts were darkened." Merriam-Webster defines *futile* as "serving no useful purpose; completely ineffective; occupied with trifles."[6] So, basically, their thinking was no longer logical, thus the usage of the word *foolish*. As humans in our rebelliousness, we claimed to "be wise" but "became fools, and exchanged the glory of the immortal God for images resembling mortal man and birds and animals and creeping things" (vv. 22–23). How insane! It's like saying, "I don't like this diamond ring I have. In fact, I don't believe a diamond is valuable or that it even exists. I'm going to throw it away and wear a string around my finger instead. This string is so much more beautiful and valuable than that diamond ring! This string is a treasure!" WHAT? That doesn't even make sense! But this is, in fact, what has happened!

Throughout the remainder of this passage we see the decline of mankind spiral further and further out of control. Every aspect of life is fair game in rebellion:

> "They were filled with all manner of unrighteousness, evil, covetousness, malice. They are full of envy, murder, strife, deceit, maliciousness. They are gossips, slanderers, haters of God, insolent, haughty, boastful, inventors of evil, disobedient to parents, foolish, faithless, heartless, ruthless" (vv. 29–31).

Why yes, this describes the world perfectly. The world is filled with people whose character is just like this.

---

[6] "futile." *Merriam-Webster.com*. 2019. https://www.merriam-webster.com (20 Feb 2019).

Friends, our world is broken. This is no secret. It is broken because of the rampant and unchecked sin in our hearts. It is evil because of the millions who are shaking their fists in rebellion against God. Not only is the individual doomed and hopeless in their sin, but our world is as well. James says, "You adulterous people! Do you not know that friendship with the world is enmity with God?" (4:4). The world is at odds with God and has been ever since the fall.

Praise God the story does not end here! Brothers and sisters, we have a Savior! And his name is Jesus! The heaviness and hopelessness of sin makes Jesus that much sweeter! Paul reminds the Roman church of this hope in Romans 6:23: "For the wages of sin is death, but the free gift of God is eternal life in Christ Jesus our Lord." The Apostle Peter proclaimed this same hope to the Jewish leaders: "This Jesus is the stone that was rejected by you, the builders, which has become the cornerstone. And there is salvation in no one else, for there is no other name under heaven given among men by which we must be saved" (Acts 4:11–12).

Though we were dead in our sins and in outright rebellion against God, he made a way of reconciliation for us through his Son, Christ Jesus! John 3:16–17 tells us, "For God so loved the world, that he gave his only Son, that whoever believes in him should not perish but have eternal life. For God did not send his son into the world to condemn the world, but in order that the world might be saved through him." How did he do this? As prophesied by the prophet Isaiah: "he was pierced for our transgressions; he was crushed for our iniquities; upon him was the chastisement that brought us peace, and with his wounds we are healed" (Isaiah 53:5). He died for you, beloved; "He was delivered over to death for our sins and was raised to life for our justification" (Romans 4:25 NIV). Jesus himself proclaimed, "I am the way, and the truth, and the life. No one comes to the Father except through me" (John 14:6). What incredible news! There is hope! This is the good news of salvation, *the only* solution.

Dear friends, let me go further and remind you of *who* Jesus is and what he offers. In John 10:1–21, Jesus describes himself as the good shepherd. He starts by saying, "he calls his own sheep by name and leads them out" (v. 3). Think about that. Jesus *knows* his sheep, and they know him. He calls *you*, specifically you. This is a personal call. He is not calling the crowd, but each individual by name. What hope for the unbeliever! Not only is Jesus the remedy for our hopeless state, He is personally invested in each individual.

Jesus doesn't stop at calling us. He offers what we most long for: abundant life and freedom. In verses 9–10 he says, "I am the door. If anyone enters by me, he will be saved and will go in and out and find pasture . . . I came *that they may have life and have it abundantly*" (author's emphasis). Jesus offers freedom. He says, "he will be saved and will go in and out." This is a picture of mobility, not being limited to the pasture. However, though he offers freedom, Jesus still offers the pasture. This implies that he will give you rest, peace, and safety and will provide for your needs, which is the purpose of a pasture. He also promises an abundant life. This means the life you live following Jesus will be large, plentiful, lavish, copious, and rich. Is this not the life we all strive for? Is this not what we all long for in the core of who we are?

I love that Jesus describes himself as a *good* shepherd. It reveals a character that is strong, brave, and mighty but tender. This is who is calling you to follow him. He wants to care for your soul. He says,

> "Come to me, all who labor and are heavy laden, and I will give you rest. Take my yoke upon you, and learn from me, for I am gentle and lowly in heart, and you will find rest for your souls" (Matthew 11:28–29).

This is the good news- that there is a remedy for our hopeless situation, and his name is Jesus. He sacrificed himself that we might be reconciled to God.[7] He is good. He offers and has the ability to give you an abundant life, and he will treat you tenderly. What does he want in return? He wants you to follow him. To know him. To know his voice and come when he calls.

With how heavy a note we ended on in the last chapter, I hope you are now soaring with the hope of the good news of Jesus Christ. Friends, this is why we are different from the world! And this is what our patients long for and crave, but do not have. Brothers and sisters, I pray that you will not keep the good news of salvation from those who need it most. Today, ask the Lord for boldness and proclaim what he has done, for it is incredible!

---

[7] 2 Corinthians 5:18

"I Have Overcome the World"

For we ourselves were once foolish, disobedient, led astray, slaves to various passions and pleasures, passing our days in malice and envy, hated by others and hating one another. But when the goodness and loving kindness of God our Savior appeared, he saved us, not because of works done by us in righteousness, but according to his own mercy, by the washing of regeneration and renewal of the Holy Spirit, whom he poured out on us richly through Jesus Christ our Savior, so that being justified by his grace we might become heirs according to the hope of eternal life.

Titus 3:3–7

Of all the behavioral health cases that come through our unit, the most sickening and heart-wrenching are the ones with histories of extensive abuse. Many of this population have known abuse since early toddlerhood or kindergarten. The years of abuse take their toll, and they create in people a warped, twisted, and broken understanding of themselves and the world around them. There are two cases in particular that always come to mind: two girls from very similar circumstances with two vastly different responses. Both girls had been abused from a sickeningly young age, both had been in and out of the foster care system, both were on a trajectory for a short and tragic life. One was being trafficked and heard truth spoken to her but in her hardness of heart refused to be saved. The other heard the call of Jesus on her life and was changed in an instant. Within the next twenty-hour hours everyone around her could tell there was something different about her, and in conversation there was already evidence of the Holy Spirit at work in her heart.

As I look on at the darkness that invades my patients' lives, my heart screams over and over, "God where are you? God how can this be fixed?" But he reminds me, "Take heart; I have overcome the world" (John 16:33). What encouragement and hope! Not just for my own heart and peace of mind, but for my patients'! The tenderness that pours from this verse is incredible! Not only is Jesus declaring what is true about himself in his statement—"I have overcome the world"—but he is demonstrating that he cares when his creation is downtrodden. He cares to speak into our lives and call us. He cares to save us, and he cares to guide our lives. Praise God and rest in this, dear friends! This is the God you serve, who called you and whom you are following!

Before we go any further, I would like to dive a little deeper into this verse. We only barely scratched the surface. There is still so much more to glean from these few words. Here is the entirety of John 16:33: "I have said these things to you, that in me you may have peace. In the world you will have tribulation. But take heart; I have overcome the world." In the preceding verses, Jesus is telling his disciples of what is coming—his betrayal and their scattering before his crucifixion. He knew it would be hard for them. He knew they would be confused and in turmoil. So, he speaks ahead of their turmoil to give them peace and hope. Two things we know for certain from this verse. First, in this broken world we *will* have hardships and difficulties. And second, *he has overcome the world*!

Let's hone in on that second half of the verse. The Greek word used for "take heart" is *tharseo,* which means to be courageous or cheer up. This word is either spoken by Jesus himself or spoken in reference to Jesus.[1] In Matthew 9:2, Jesus heals a paralytic and says, "Take heart,

---

[1] Louis A. Barbieri, et al., *The Bible Knowledge Commentary: New Testament*, ed. John F. Walvoord and Roy B. Zuck (Colorado Springs: Cook Communications Ministries, 1983).

my son; your sins are forgiven." In Matthew 9:22, Jesus heals a woman of a bleeding disorder and says, "Take heart, daughter; your faith has made you well." In Matthew 14:27, Jesus' disciples are afraid at the sight of a figure walking on the water to them, and Jesus calls out to them, "Take heart; it is I. Do not be afraid." In Mark 10:46–49, we see Jesus respond to a poor, blind beggar who is crying for help. Not hearing Jesus, the crowd tells him, "Take heart. Get up; he is calling you." And finally, in Acts 23:11, the Lord reveals his plans for Paul when he tells him, "Take courage [heart], for as you have testified to the facts about me in Jerusalem, so you must testify also in Rome."

What do all these verses and stories tell us? They tell us, *take heart*, beloved! Jesus heals and repairs, even the impossible. He saves. *Take heart*, he is here and we do not have to be bound by or consumed by fear. *Take heart*, he is calling YOU. *Take heart*, he has a purpose for your life and he knows your future! This is hope for us, yes, but this is hope for our peers and patients too! We do not need to tell them, "Keep calm and carry on," because that little pat saying is hopeless and devoid of life. Rather, we can speak into their darkness and say, "Take heart, Jesus is calling you, and he is big enough to care for you, and he sees you."

I want to encourage you as a child of the King! He knows your future and created you for a purpose, and, friend, his love is immense. In Romans 8, Paul reminds us, "Who shall separate us from the love of Christ? Shall tribulation, or distress, or persecution, or famine, or nakedness, or danger, or sword? . . . No, in all things we are more than conquerors through *him who loved us*. For I am sure that neither death nor life, nor angels nor rulers, nor things present nor things to come, nor powers, nor height nor depth, *nor anything else in all creation*, will be able to separate us from the love of God in Christ Jesus our Lord" (vv. 35, 37–39, author's emphasis). Remember that the love of the Lord is deep. It is like an ocean. Who can count its drops? As the depths of the ocean are unknown, so are the depths of the Father's love. Drown in it, beloved.

The Father's Love

When God called the nation of Israel out of Egypt, he promised this love: "The LORD, the LORD, a God merciful and gracious, slow to anger, and abounding in steadfast love and faithfulness, keeping steadfast love for thousands, forgiving iniquity and transgression and sin" (Exodus 34:6–7). In Hebrew, *hesed* is the word used for steadfast love, or loyal love,[2] the same kind of love as between a husband and wife.[3] God is faithful in his love, though we are not. In response to Israel's (and our) repeated unfaithfulness, he pursues and tenderly tells us, "I have loved you with an everlasting love; therefore I have continued my faithfulness to you" (Jeremiah 31:3).

Brother, sister, God loves you. He will fight for you and conquer the world for you, and you can rest assured of these promises because he tenderly and carefully created you. He purposefully crafted you; your existence is not by chance! David proclaims this truth in Psalm 139:13–16:

> For you formed my inward parts; you knitted me together in my mother's womb. I praise you, for I am fearfully and wonderfully made. Wonderful are your works; my soul knows it very well. My frame was not hidden from you, when I was being made in secret, intricately woven in the depths of the earth. Your eyes saw my unformed substance; in your book were written, every one of them, the days that were formed for me, when as yet there was none of them.

He knows you through and through. He knows you better than you know you. You are not living life on your own, and God is not distant. He has not walked away. In fact, he is inescapable![4] He is here. He is right in the thick of life with you!

Why am I reminding you of our hope in Christ as believers? Why is it important to remember these truths? We must remember these biblical truths because a better understanding and a consistent reminder of who God is and what he daily does for us should change and shape us. Friend, we should be strikingly different from our non-believing friends, patients, and co-workers! Not only do we have freedom and life while they are bound in death, we have a loving and good God who daily

---

[2] Louis A. Barbieri, et al., The Bible Knowledge Commentary: New Testament (1983) 158.

[3] John Piper, "The Meanings of Love in the Bible," (Desiring God, 1975).

[4] Psalm 139:7–12

drenches us in his love, who fights victoriously for us and intentionally created us for specific purposes!

I love that the Lord loves us deeply. His love gives me hope and shines in my darkness. 2 Corinthians 4:6 proclaims this truth: "For God, who said, 'Let light shine out of darkness,' has shone in our hearts to give the light of the knowledge of the glory of God in the face of Jesus Christ." This light, this hope, should radiate from us! It should be bright and its origin unmistakable, because God Almighty loves us and is faithful in his love.

In the following verses Paul expounds on how the light of Christ in our hearts should shape our lives:

> But we have this treasure in jars of clay, to show that the surpassing power belongs to God and not to us. We are afflicted in every way, but not crushed; perplexed, but not driven to despair; persecuted, but not forsaken; struck down, but not destroyed . . . *So we do not lose heart*. Though our outer self is wasting away, our inner self is being renewed day by day." (vv. 7–9, 16 author's emphasis)

Did you catch that phrase? "So we do not lose heart." It rings of Jesus' encouragement to *take heart*. It is the hope of Jesus that propels us, shapes us, and carries us through the good and the bad.

Are you burnt-out and weary from this job that threatens to steal your heart and wither your soul? Cling to Christ! Search for him, because he has the hope, that breath of air you are swimming desperately toward the surface for. Is your patient suffering and your own heart echoing their cry to God for answers and respite? Does the darkness seem too dark, the world too heavy, and the way impossible? Do not lose heart! Jesus is coming and is as faithful to come as the sun dawning on the horizon. Run to him and experience his warm love as it washes over you, your patients, your peers, and your life.

God's Grace

Another facet of God's immense love is his grace. The letters that the apostles wrote to the early church remind us "by grace [we] have been saved" (Ephesians 2:8) and though we fail in our pursuit and commitment to God, "he gives more grace" (James 4:6). By those truths alone we are drowning in his grace! Yet, his loving grace extends even further! In Paul's second letter to the Corinthian church, he shares how he struggled with weakness but the Lord spoke into his struggle and said, "My grace is sufficient for you, for my power is made perfect in weakness" (12:9). We then hear how Paul was changed by the Lord's abounding grace in his life. Before, he was focused on his circumstances[5], but after, his eyes were set on Christ's power in his life and he was no longer consumed by his circumstances. Friend, don't obsess over your inadequacies and weaknesses. The Lord has you where he has you for a reason. His grace is sufficient for you. Instead, trust his power as it is at work in your life overcoming your weaknesses.

Since we are commanded to live in God's grace and love, what does that practically look like? In Galatians, Paul spells it out for us: "But the fruit of the Spirit is love, joy, peace, patience, kindness, goodness, faithfulness, gentleness, self-control; against such things there is no law" (5:22–23). Throughout the Bible God frequently uses trees and fruit as metaphors for life, growth, and the inner workings of the heart. I think it paints such a good picture of what is happening under the surface. For any plant to bear fruit, the plant must have a lot of water, nutrients, and sunlight. Without those things, there will be no fruit. Without fruit, the fruit-bearing plant may be alive, but it is not living to its full purpose and potential. So it is with us. If we are not letting God sustain us, feed us, and grow us, we will not bear spiritual fruit. A heart that lets the light and love of Jesus shine through it will bear fruit, as it is living life or "keeping in step" with the Holy Spirit.[6]

Again, in Paul's first letter to the Corinthian church, he describes what a life shaped by Christ's love looks like:

> Love is patient and kind; love does not envy or boast; it is not arrogant or rude. It does not insist on its own way; it is not irritable or resentful; it does not rejoice in wrongdoing, but rejoices with the truth. Love bears all things, believes all things, hopes all things, endures all things. (1 Corinthians 13:4–7)

I don't know about you, but this passage is way more humbling than the passage in Galatians! How often I fall short and emulate unloving characteristics rather than these!

---

[5] 2 Corinthians 12:7–8
[6] Galatians 5:25

Let me make the argument that we are in a unique position. As followers of Jesus, we can serve and love our patients, friends, and coworkers in ways that others simply cannot. The rest of the world is bound in selfish sin and death. They cannot see as Jesus does; they are blind. As Luke 6:39 puts it, "Can a blind man lead a blind man? Will they not both fall into a pit?" We, however, are different! The God of the universe has called us, spoken into our lives, and changed us. He made us new when we accepted his Son as our Savior. His power, righteousness, life, and love are at work within our hearts and shine out like a city on a hill.[7] We actually have the tools and ability to meet our patients' needs, not because of what we can do or who we are, but because of HIM who is in us!

Learning to Love Like the Father

Using what we have been given is not optional. Brothers and sisters, we are instructed to serve. In John 13:13–15 Jesus, after washing his disciples' feet (something a servant would do), asks if they understand what he is trying to teach them. He says, "You call me Teacher and Lord, and you are right, for so I am. If I then, your Lord and Teacher, have washed your feet, you also ought to wash one another's feet. For I have given you an example, that you also should do just as I have done to you." Your Lord and Savior was ready and willing to serve, just as He does now. So you should be as well.

Allow me to be vulnerable with you for a moment. The place where God has put me in my career is not where I wanted to be, nor is it a place I would have ever chosen. But I cannot deny that His hand has moved me to this position. During the past couple of years I looked for a new job and prayed for the Lord to provide one. Throughout this time he told me, "No. Stay. This is where I have put you. This is where I want you." That was not the response I was hoping and waiting for. Patiently and unwearyingly he carried me through hardship and some very toddler-like temper tantrums to get me to the point where I was willing to joyfully serve him where he has placed me. And now I am confronted with a new reality: what if this placement (that I had assumed would be a temporary season) is actually a permanent calling? What if God is

---

[7] Matthew 5:14

calling me to a role and career that I don't necessarily like, that is emotionally exhausting and spiritually dark?

In John chapter 6, Jesus discusses some very controversial and difficult issues, causing may of his followers to turn away and stop walking with him.[8] Jesus then turns to the twelve apostles, his closest and dearest friends, and asks them, "Do you want to go away as well?" (v. 67). The apostle Peter responds, "Lord, to whom shall we go? You have the words of eternal life, and we have believed, and have come to know, that you are the Holy One of God" (vv. 68–69). Friends, I have struggled deeply and some days continue to struggle with the purpose God has for me and the path he has me on, but where will I go without him? Who compares? I will gladly follow him though I might not like the path or though he leads me through the valley of the shadow of death, because he is with me! How could I walk away from him?

I want to challenge you today to look at your life and take stock. Are you frustrated and dissatisfied with the path the Lord has you on? Do you love him enough to stick with him, though the road is long and difficult? Or will you turn away and miss out on a lifetime of abundance and rest in the shadow of his wing? Oh, beloved, I pray you will choose him! He is worth it!

> *The LORD is my shepherd; I shall not want.*
> *He makes me lie down in green pastures.*
> *He leads me beside still waters.*
> *He restores my soul.*
> *He leads me in paths of righteousness*
> *for his name's sake.*
> *Even though I walk through the shadow of death,*
> *I will fear no evil,*
> *for you are with me;*
> *your rod and your staff,*
> *they comfort me.*
> *Psalm 23:1–4*

---

[8] John 6:66

Physically Sick Souls

The hardest lesson the Lord ever taught me came through a patient I took care of for years named Melody. Melody was manipulative, a compulsive liar, stubborn, and prone to fits of anger. She loved pushing people around and was not afraid to throw her weight around to get her way. I could not stand her. There was definitely a clash of personalities between us, and I was determined not to be manipulated by her. I often responded in frustration to her infuriating behavior and could be harsh and unloving with her. Now I look back and see the hardness of my heart and lack of a Christ-like attitude and it saddens me. Melody was lonely and broken. She had chased away friends, and even her own parents couldn't bear to be around her. They would leave her alone in the hospital for weeks at a time.

Melody spiraled further and further down the drain and ended up passing away in her teens. She had finally succumbed to the long-term strain her body had endured from years of non-compliance. In the adult world, it is easy to point a finger at someone and attribute his or her illness to choices made in life. In Melody's case, this was not so easy. Yes, she had been non-compliant, but she was also just a kid who'd had very little parental support and guidance. Her illness and subsequent death were horrible, especially because they could have been prevented. There is something awful about a child dying that leaves you overwhelmed with questions and that stirs the deep, unshakable thought that this is very wrong.

As healthcare professionals we are always looking to understand, always digging to answer the question, what is the root cause? Even Jesus' disciples struggled to understand the overwhelming volume of illnesses that they saw when they walked with Jesus. On one occasion they came across a man who had been blind from birth, and they asked Jesus, "Rabbi, who sinned, this man or his parents, that he was born blind?" (John 9:2). Their question reflects our longing to understand.

When I think of heartbreaking illness, I think of the many patients I have cared for over the years who have been diagnosed with cancers, devastating meningitis, uncontrollable autism, and unexpected and deadly diabetic complications. I think of those with neurofibromas that have destroyed and consumed their bodies and with PTSD from years of abuse. And as I think of each of these individuals, my emotions threaten to spill over. As you know, there will always be specific patients you think about often and who weigh heavy on your heart. It is these patients who pushed me to understand God's Word better, that the Lord might use me to shine light into their darkness.

Hope found in Scripture

So, why? Why do our patients suffer? Why are they dealt such devastating blows? There is actually *a lot* of scripture on illness, and I would encourage you to study the Word on your own so that through it the Lord can give you deeper understanding.

The Bible clearly talks about the root causes of illness, though I think we have often missed these references in our Bible studies. We will explore where the Bible talks about these root causes, which are: sinful behavior, living in a broken and decaying world, rejecting God, the testing of one's faith and bringing glory to God, and demonic and satanic oppression and possession.

Come, let's wrestle through this hard topic and see what God's Word says. I think you will find, as I have, that the Bible has much to say about illness, and we will see in the next chapter that the Bible has a lot to say about healing and hope. I'm not saying that we need to throw our brains out of the equation and rely on faith alone. What I am saying is an echo of what God reminds us in Jeremiah 33. He created this world with intention and beautiful purpose. He has full, intimate knowledge of the world and our bodies as Creator and Sovereign. We should be looking to him as the source of all knowledge, to fill the gaps of our understanding. Are you so caught up with the physical that you are blind the underlying spiritual issues?

You don't have to be a genius to know that there is more to us than merely our physical bodies. In religions around the world and outlets like movies and mainstream music, the soul and spirit of a person are constantly being explored. Even in our nursing and medical schools the spiritual wellbeing of a person is highlighted as an important aspect of physical wellness. We must strive to understand the whole person, and we have the ability to fully do so through God's Word. "Call to me," God says, "and I will answer you, and will tell you great and hidden things that you have not known" (Jeremiah 33:3).

Let's begin our exploration with the incredible story of one of the most well-known characters of the Bible, Job. Job was struck with horrible sickness, lasting years. As he struggled through brokenness, depression, loss, and disease, he wrestled with the spiritual aspect of mankind, as did his friends (who decided to give their "two cents" on his situation). One man said to him, "But it is the *spirit* in man, the breath of the Almighty, that makes him understand" (Job 32:8). Then later in 33:4 he says, "The Spirit of God has made me, and the breath of the Almighty gives me life." In the man's commentary on Job's situation, he reminds both Job and the reader that our souls and our bodies are one. Our physical minds and spiritual souls were created by God to be you and me. We are bodies, made of cells and synapses, but we are also alive, by God's grace, with cognitive functionality, personality, and a will. We are spiritual because God has breathed life into us.

We know that this world is broken, and both mental illness and physical illness are proof that death reigns in our bodies. In Romans 5:12, Paul says, "death spread to all men because all sinned." He builds on this idea a few chapters later when he says, "For we know that the whole creation has been groaning together in the pains of childbirth until now" (8:22). He is not saying that we are all literally giving birth, but that we feel the horrible, painful effects of sin. Sin affects our physical being as much as it affects our soul, because we are a part of creation. Again, in 2 Corinthians 4:16, Paul talks about our "outer self . . . wasting away." This statement merely solidifies what we know to be true: that we are dying, every day, from the moment of conception. Humanity is dynamic, growing and changing throughout our lives, but decaying with every breath, every moment. In cancer our bodies groan, in schizophrenia our minds groan, and in response our hearts groan with longing for the healing, restoration, freedom, and reconciliation Jesus offers.

Through multiple accounts of healing in the Gospels, there appears to be a trend of people who were sick for no other apparent reason than that they lived in our sin-filled, dying world. In Matthew 12:9–13, Jesus encounters a man who has a withered hand and heals him in front of the religious elite. In Matthew 9:18–25, we read of a girl who has died from unknown causes and a woman with a bleeding disorder from which she has suffered for many years. Jesus heals them both, raising the girl from the dead and stopping the bleeding of the woman. Jesus meets two blind men in Matthew 20:29–34. He sees their value though others do not and restores their sight. In Mark 1:30–31 he heals a woman of fever, and just a few lines down, in verses 40–42, he heals a man of leprosy.

This is in line with what we observe today. Not all ailments and illness are attributable to one particular reason. Many of us have seen many idiopathic disease processes wreak havoc on good and kind people. There is no explainable reason why my brother was diagnosed with Ewing's sarcoma at thirteen years old. Or why my twenty-seven-year-old co-worker was diagnosed with aggressive breast cancer. We often lack reason for what caused diabetes in a six-year-old patient, or ichtheyosis, or SLE, or any one of so many other horrible, painful, debilitating maladies.

Notice, though, that in each of Jesus' accounts with the sick, it didn't necessarily matter what had caused the affliction. Jesus had power over it all. From incurable and chronic skin infections, to unexplainable hemorrhaging, to deformity, to death, there was not one person Jesus was unable to heal. Beloved, humanity has suffered through the ages because our world is broken, and Jesus has the power to heal it all. Just because our efforts fail does not mean God is powerless.

For God's Glory

I also want to point out that there are also several occasions in the Bible when Jesus healed people and indicated that it was their faith that healed them. One of these instances, in Matthew 9:20–22, is a story we briefly mentioned a moment ago. This is the woman who had a bleeding disorder, characterized by bloody discharge, for twelve years.

It was in faith that she sought Jesus. It was in faith that she stretched out her hand hoping that merely brushing his clothes with her fingers would heal her. And it was in faith that this woman confessed that she sought healing though Jesus.

God uses our faith to bring himself glory. Nowhere else is this more clearly portrayed than in the life and suffering of Job. At the beginning of the book of Job, we see Satan approach God accusing Job of being less than what God claims he is—"a blameless and upright man" (Job 2:3). In response to this accusation, God allows Job to be stripped of his family, wealth, and health, keeping only his life. Not once through his years of suffering does Job curse God and sin, though he does ask a lot of questions. At the end of this period of hardship, because of his faithfulness to God, Job's health is restored and he becomes even more prosperous and experiences even greater blessings. His faith brought glory to God and demonstrated that God does, indeed, know the heart of man.

However, not all spiritual testing results in strengthened faith. In 2 Chronicles 16:10–13, we see King Asa develop a disease in both of his feet. Though he was considered a "good" king who served the Lord, his heart had become prideful and hard, and he was prone to self-reliance. God allowed him to struggle with this illness to give him an easy opportunity to turn back to him. This is not what happened, though: "Yet even in his disease he did not seek the LORD, but sought help from physicians" (v. 12). King Asa died in self-reliance. His lack of trust in God prolonged his suffering, and the text implies that he died because of his lack of faith.

These are all interesting accounts, but how else does God use illness to bring himself glory? In John 9 we see Jesus encounter a man who was born blind. When they see the man, Jesus' disciples ask, "Rabbi, who sinned, this man or his parents, that he was born blind?" (v. 2). Jesus responds, "It was not that this man sinned, or his parents, *but that the works of God might be displayed in him*" (v. 3, author's emphasis). What an interesting statement. God allowed that this man be born blind so that through his miraculous healing God's power would be proven.

Look a little further down in the chapter to verses 35–37. Now the excitement has died down and the religious leaders have expelled the man in contempt, and Jesus asks him, "Do you believe in the Son of Man?" The man's response? He has no idea who Jesus is talking about! He has no idea that the Messiah, God incarnate, is the one who healed him! It is only when Jesus reveals himself as the Messiah to the previously blind man that he believes! Friends, God allows for some people to struggle with illness and debilitating disease so that His name will be glorified through their healing AND to save their souls from destruction! He is God, but do not mistake God's sovereign and gracious plan for callousness. Yes, he is using this man's life of hardship to bring himself glory, but he is also calling him personally. God was never blind to his blindness but intentionally allowed it for an incredible outcome! He became the walking embodiment of God's miraculous work to rescue and restore humanity.

Then, in John 11, there is the incredible story of Lazarus. This awe-inspiring account reveals to us a great deal about God the Father and Jesus the Beloved. In verses 2–6 word is sent to Jesus that Lazarus, a dear friend, is deathly ill. Jesus then delays *two more days* before going to meet Lazarus. Jesus clearly knows that Lazarus is not just sick but on his deathbed, so why does he delay? He delays so that God's plan will be fulfilled, thus brining God glory.[1] Sometimes God chooses not to rescue us out of *possible* situations because when he rescues us out of *impossible* situations he is glorified even more and our faith is deepened in ways it might not have been otherwise.

In verses 17–38 of chapter 11, we see an urgency and intentionality in Jesus during moments of grief. As he approaches Lazarus' tomb, he is twice overcome by emotion. The phrase used in the text to describe how Jesus felt in these moments is "deeply moved" (vv. 33, 38), which in the Greek connotes indignation, anger, or sternness. Picture this, Jesus is overcome with emotion in response to the grief around him and the sight of his good friend dead and buried, but it is not merely sorrow and loss that he is feeling so deeply. Jesus sees things more clearly than we do, and his indignation and anger came from a full understanding of the toll of sin on an individual, which results in illness and death.[2] Did you catch what I'm trying to point out to you? Jesus groaned and struggled with brokenness as we do! Jesus mourns and hates the loss of life and the wages of sin, which are ultimately death. Beloved, rest assured, God sees your patients in their brokenness, on

[1] Louis A. Barbieri, et al., The Bible Knowledge Commentary: New Testament (1983) 313.

[2] Louis A. Barbieri, et al., The Bible Knowledge Commentary: New Testament (1983) 314.

their deathbeds, in their illness, and is deeply moved by their state. He hates death, because it is evidence of the hold that sin has on this world.

Read on in John 11. Next, being moved in righteous indignation over the broken order of his creation, Jesus commands that the stone be rolled away and prays aloud for all to hear, "Father, I thank you that you have heard me. I knew that you always hear me, but I said this on account of the people standing around, that they may believe that you sent me" (vv. 41–42). And then he looked in at that dark, foul-smelling, decay-filled tomb and cried out loudly, "Lazarus, come out" (v. 43). And incredibly, the four-day dead man came out walking. Friends, let's aim to be more like Jesus, who seized the opportunity of grief to point the people around him to God. He broke with them, feeling the full weight of their sorrow, loss, and sin, and did not stop there. Even in grief Jesus was working to reconcile people back to the Father. We too must be so tender and empathetic and still just as intentional. This is a very hard thing to do, and our Savior does it perfectly. Let us look to Christ as our example!

The Sin Spiral

In Lazarus' story we encounter Jesus' indignant, righteous response to death, which we know to be a product of sin reigning in creation. Now we will explore how illness can be directly caused by sin. This concept, however, is very broad. We can further subcategorize illness caused by sin into three categories: illnesses as a result of personal sin, illnesses due to generational sin or parental sin, and illness resulting from collective or national sin.

First, let us look at illnesses that come from personal sin. Initially, this category seems to be the most straightforward. We will likely all agree that indulging in vices tends to have bad outcomes. Anyone could make the argument that alcoholism can cause cirrhosis of the liver. Sexual promiscuity and "unsafe sex practices" tend to lead to STDs. Years of smoking generally lead to lung cancers, and gluttony often causes fatty liver, diabetes, and heart disease. However, in Mark 2:1–12 we see Jesus heal a *paralytic* after telling him that his *sins were forgiven*.

In the account, we are not privy to what sins Jesus was referring to, but it would seem that his paralysis was attributed to his sin. In the Old Testament, King Jehoram of Judah murdered his brothers, rejected

God, and led his whole country away from God into immorality and idol worship. He was struck with a "disease of [his] bowels" (2 Chronicles 21:15) that eventually led to a prolapse of his bowels, while his family was struck with a severe plague, *because of his great sin*. After two years of suffering, he "died in great agony" at only forty years old (v. 19). Also, in James 5:15 we see sickness tied to sin. James urges the early church to confess their sins to each other and pray for each other so that they can be healed. This implies that their sickness was caused by unrepentant sin in their lives.

Often our personal and habitual sins get passed on to the next generation. It is the mystery of children repeating the sins of their parents. This is not a foreign concept to us. We know well that the abused tend to become abusers in turn. In 2 Samuel 12, we see the prophet Nathan harshly rebuke King David for killing a man to hide his sexual sin with the man's wife. He says to David, "Why have you despised the word of the LORD, to do what is evil in his sight? You have struck down Uriah the Hittite with the sword and have taken his wife to be your wife and have killed him with the sword of the Ammonites. Now therefore the sword shall never depart from your house" (vv. 9–10).

Not only do we see Nathan's prophecy proven to be true, we see how David's sins are passed down to his children, even to the most "godly" of them, King Solomon. After David dies, Solomon proves himself to be a womanizer. He has seven *hundred* wives and three *hundred* concubines. Essentially he has ONE THOUSAND women at his disposal for his every want. These women eventually turn Solomon's heart away from God, and near the end of his life he chooses to worship idols rather than Yahweh. In response to Solomon's decision to ignore the command to wholly serve God (as King David did), God promises to all but tear the kingdom away from King Solomon's descendants.[3] From King Solomon's son, Rehoboam, down through the royal family line, we see God's promise hold true. Brothers kill each other for the throne, kings die in battle, and the kingdom is just about stripped from David's descendants.

Do you see where the trend began? It began with King David. His sons watched him sin. Solomon himself was the product of the infamously scandalous union of King David and Bathsheba. Solomon

---

[3] 1 Kings 11:1–13

indulged in every pleasure known to man,[4] including the objectification of a thousand women, which was taught to him by his father and brothers. And with that bend, Solomon walked away from the Lord. His sons learned to walk away from the Lord and walk instead in sinful self-indulgence.

In Exodus 20, God warns the people of Israel that if they turn away from God and sin, he will visit "the iniquity of the fathers on the children to the third and the fourth generation" (Exodus 20:5). However, in Leviticus 26:39–42 God promises forgiveness and restoration to those who humbly turn away from their fathers' sins. This passage reveals to us that the sins that we are so prone to hold on to and pass down to our children, grandchildren, and great-grandchildren, are not hopeless. No one has to be trapped in their parents' sins or even their own sins. Through God the cycle of sin can be broken.

The history of Israel shows how an individual's sin can grow and pass on to children and grandchildren and spread before long to a whole nation. From their leaving Egypt, to their wandering in the desert, to their settling in the Promised Land, to their growing as a nation, Israel struggled repeatedly with national sin, specifically turning away from God.

In response to Israel's wayward spirit, God promises blessings on those who are faithful to follow him and curses on those who reject him.[5] According to Merriam-Webster, "a curse is a prayer of invocation of harm or injury to come upon one; evil or misfortune that comes as if in retribution; a cause of great harm or misfortune; torment."[6] God is warning the people of Israel that every aspect of their lives will be characterized by hardship, harm, and misfortune if they do not obey his voice. These curses would affect where they lived, their work and livelihood, their children, their ability to bear children, their travels, their health, their marriage, and their state of mind. He warned them that nothing would be easy and that heartache and frustration would never be far away.

God is, in fact, very specific when He describes what to expect if Israel chooses to turn away from him. In Deuteronomy 28, there are specific illnesses (plagues) that are listed, such as wasting disease, fever,

---

[4] Ecclesiastes 2:1, 8

[5] Deuteronomy 28

[6] "curse." *Merriam-Webster.com*. 2019. https://www.merriam-webster.com (22 Feb 2019).

inflammation, boils, tumors, scabs, and boils to the knees and legs. Then there are generational (inherited) illnesses, chronic illnesses, and congenital illnesses that are described as grievous and lasting. Finally, mental health is also addressed in this passage. Madness, confusion, and anxiety will plague the nation if they turn away from their God. To be clear, these are illnesses that the nation as a whole would experience if, as a people, they turned away from God.

Then, in Hosea 9, verses 7–14, we see the nation of Israel reap the fruit of their sin and God carry out the curses that he warned them about. In this passage, the prophet sings a song of lament over Israel. He says that the nation has turned away from God; fathers have led their children away from life to death. In response, God has plagued the nation with infertility and miscarriage. And even the small number of children who are born will die. It is a horrible picture of the consequences God's people face when they choose to be unfaithful to God. Reading these warnings in the Bible has caused me to stop and consider, how much of the illness I see at work is a consequence of generational and national sin?

As a people, Israel came to a place of hopelessness, discouragement, death, loss, confusion, anxiety, and insanity because they walked away from their Source of abundant life. If sin is so degenerative to life, causing decay in its wake, it seems only logical that everything in life will decay apart from Christ. Reason, cognition, hormones, organs, tissues, chemicals, spirit, and soul, all touched by the black death of sin. And when sin is rampant, the nations groan in loss and agony.

Spiritual Forces

The last root of illness I would like to touch on is demonic and satanic oppression and possession. I have eased into this last category because Western culture is so determined to be ignorant of mysterious, unseen forces, though they are addressed throughout the Bible. In a couple of chapters we will discuss at length Satan and demons and how they influence our lives and the lives of our patients, but I would like to highlight a few passages of Scripture here that clearly point to these dark, spiritual forces as the cause of some instances of illness.

Recall that in Job 2 Satan comes before God to accuse Job and in response *God allows* Satan to cause sores to erupt all over Job's body, from his head down to his feet. God also permits Satan to take the lives of Job's family members, but he cannot take Job's. Satan therefore *does* have the power to harm people and take human life, but only as a dog on a leash. All he can do is only what God allows.

In Matthew 12, Jesus comes upon a man possessed by a demon *credited with causing blindness and dysphasia.* Accordingly, when Jesus heals the man, he is able to see and talk. In Matthew 17, Jesus heals a demon-possessed boy whose demon *caused him to have epilepsy.* And in Mark 9, Jesus heals yet another boy possessed by a demon, and this one Jesus addresses as "You mute and deaf spirit" (v. 25), implying that *this demon caused deafness and dysphasia in the boy.* I'm showing you these passages to challenge your worldview. There are invisible (to us) spiritual forces that are at work against us to keep humanity trapped and hopeless in sin. However, Jesus has power over them all. From Satan himself to multitudes of demons, they all are subject to our Lord, whether they like it or not. There is not one illness, malady, injury, or disease that Jesus Christ is powerless against.

Friends, this chapter has been such a challenge. I have at times felt like I am drowning in scripture. Though it is a lot of information to process, I pray that as you reflect on the scripture we covered you would allow the Holy Spirit to challenge your current worldview. I pray that the Lord would give you eyes to see your patients and their struggles. I hope that as you wrestle (as I have) with how to fit this new and broader understanding of illness into your patient care, you would seek the Lord in his Word. The Lord knows the hearts and motives of your patients. He knows the roots of their illnesses and their deep struggles. Pray and ask the Lord how you might effectively serve him in your patients' lives.

5

Healer and Restorer

The first time my husband went home with me to Indonesia was the Christmas before we married. Apart from going on a family vacation to the Virgin Islands, he had never travelled outside of the continental US. The onslaught of smells, sounds, and people in the capital city were at times overwhelming to him. I will spare you the potty humor that comes with being in a developing country, but I think it's safe to say that his world was rocked!

One particular memory that stands out was his first visit to an outdoor market. We had chosen this particular outdoor market because it was known to have some of the best textiles and stationary the city had to offer to those on a budget. He had recently asked for my hand in marriage, and had I joyfully said yes, so we tried to save money by purchasing as much as we could in Indonesia to bring back to the US for our wedding.

The morning was a typical Jakarta morning—humid, traffic-congested, and smoggy. Our driver dropped us off at the entrance, and we walked through the gate, passing a blind beggar as we entered. For me, this was life. We went from store to store to kiosk, looking for the goods that would best fit our needs. In my mind, this was the best outdoor market to bring a "first-timer." There was no food being sold in the area we were visiting, so the smells, in my mind, were not too bad. Unfortunately, I was completely oblivious to my husband-to-be. Had I paid attention, I would have seen he was drowning in culture shock. Not only had we passed a blind man begging for money, but we passed many people with various ailments. There was one person with a humongous goiter, another with odd burns, several other blind people, and a woman covered from head to toe in small, round tumors, which I would later come to know was likely neurofibromatosis. After a long day of shopping, we made it home and started talking about the whole experience. My then fiancé told me that he felt like he had been in "Bible times, but with cars." His response still makes me chuckle. His world had been rocked indeed.

Friends, I have made a career out of dealing with sickness. I might not know all the normal milestones of childhood, but I can tell you instantly if something is abnormal. After years of living in a developing country, years of training to be a nurse, and almost a decade of practicing as a bedside nurse, I cannot imagine a life with no illness of any kind. And until I die or Jesus returns, I will not know what that life looks like. However, I do know this with confidence: we have hope in Jesus Christ, because he has the power to heal and restore and in him all things are made new.

Throughout the Gospels we see Jesus heal all kinds of diseases, some of which we touched on in the previous chapter. Jesus revealed through healing that he has power over all disease, pain, and, deformity. He proved that he even has power over death when he raised Lazarus from the dead. We learned too that he has power over demons by the accounts of his freeing people from their possession. Finally, in Matthew 9, Jesus shows us that he has the power and authority to forgive and restore, curing even the evil heart of man.

When we read about Jesus' ministry in Matthew 9:35, we see that he proclaimed the gospel *and* he healed every disease and affliction. Perhaps that is the key. It is the merging of meeting peoples' spiritual needs and meeting their physical needs. Let me make the argument that to meet the physical needs of a patient the spiritual needs must be met as well. You never see Jesus heal without pointing people to God the Father and meeting their spiritual needs. I wonder if we lack effectiveness in our patient care because we are not sharing the gospel with patients and pointing them to Jesus.

If Jesus is God and God is the Creator and ultimate Healer, then should we not look to him first and foremost to heal out patients? Jesus healed by casting out demons and forgiving sins, with fasting and praying. In every instance of healing or restoration God was glorified. Is there rampant sin in the world and in the lives of my patients? Yes. Do we live in a broken world? Yes. BUT Jesus has power over the elements, as seen in Luke 8:22–25. Jesus has power over death, as seen in John 11:38–44. He has power over demons and power over sickness. There is nothing in this world that he has not proven his power and authority over.

In Psalm 103:2–5, King David says of the Lord,

> Bless the LORD, O my soul,
>   and forget not all his benefits,
> who forgives all your iniquity,
>   who heals all your diseases,
> who redeems your life from the pit,
>   who crowns you with steadfast love and mercy,
> who satisfies you with good,
>   so that your youth is renewed like the eagle's.

I think David has given us a picture of what God is doing. This is what he longs to do in our lives as well as in the lives of our patients. You see, he *forgives* your wickedness and sin. He *heals* your diseases, all of them. He *redeems*, or buys back, your life. He ransomed it from the pit. He *crowns* you with faithful love and mercy worthy of wearing proudly and showing off to the world. And he *satisfies* you with good.

Why? Why does God do all this for us? So that we will be renewed and restored to freshness and vigor, revived. Our God is in the business of healing and restoring. He wants for his creation to be who he created us to be, no longer bound by sin and death, no longer carrying the burdens of this world. This theme of restoration resounds throughout the entire Bible.

As the psalmist declares in Psalm 147:3 and 5, "He heals the brokenhearted and binds up their wounds . . . Great is our Lord, and abundant in power; his understanding is beyond measure." The Bible is filled with stories of depression, abuse, hopelessness, death, infertility, adultery, slavery, horrible families, and broken minds. But at the center of those stories is the redemption and restoration that come through God.

God is enough for our brokenness. In the life of Jesus it is revealed that God has power over sin, sickness, and evil forces. In fact, in the last chapter we discussed extensively how Jesus healed and restored people both physically and spiritually. However, I would like to challenge your understanding of God's power by showing you that *no one* is ever too far gone for God to call them, save them and restore them.

In the books of Joshua[2] and Hosea[3], God calls prostitutes, uses them for his purposes and glory, and gives them new lives. In 1 Samuel God answers the desperate prayer of a woman who struggled with infertility for years by giving her a son.[4] In Genesis God comforts a woman trapped in abuse. Though a slave, he sees her in her brokenness and gives her hope and freedom.[5] In the book of Ruth God comforts and provides for two widows, carrying them through loss, depression, and destitution. He gives them new and full lives.[6] Friends, God wants to restore, and he is tender and gentle to those who turn to Him.

God can and will speak into dark, deep depression, as he did in the life of Elijah.[7] Even a broken mind is within God's power to bring healing and restoration. In Daniel 4, God allows King Nebuchadnezzar to go through a seven-year period of insanity, clinical insanity. In verse 33 the text says, "Immediately the word was fulfilled against Nebuchadnezzar. He was driven from among men and ate grass like an ox, and his body was wet with the dew of heaven till his hair grew as long as eagles' feathers, and his nails were like birds' claws." You see, his mind was broken, but there was still hope: "At the end of the days I, Nebuchadnezzar, lifted my eyes to heaven, and my reason returned to me, and I blessed the Most High, and praised and honored him who lives forever" (v. 34). Notice, King Nebuchadnezzar's restoration did not happen until he "lifted [his] eyes to heaven"—that is, until he acknowledged God's sovereignty and authority. The point I want to make is this: *he was still able to do so with a broken mind!*

My friends, what hope is ringing out from these pages! For our friends, acquaintances, co-workers, and patients whose souls and minds

---

[2] Joshua 2 & 6:22–25

[3] Hosea 1 & 3

[4] 1 Samuel 1

[5] Genesis 38

[6] Ruth 1–4

[7] 1 Kings 19:1–18

have been broken, there is hope found in our God, through his Son, Jesus Christ! Do not believe the lie that anyone is beyond help! God can and will restore every facet of life, if we would just turn to him! God's Word is filled with stories of people's lives broken beyond repair, and God did the impossible by redeeming and restoring those people!

In Matthew 19:26 Jesus says, "With man this is impossible, but with God, all things are possible." There is *nothing* that is impossible for our God, including the healing of physical, mental, and spiritual brokenness. Beloved, this is wonderful, joyful news! We should be shouting this from the rooftops! We should be urgently and desperately sharing this hope in Jesus with as many people as possible!

Dear friend, I hope that as you remember and better understand the limitless power of our God you would pray and ask the Lord to show you how he can use you! Pray for opportunities and boldness to share the good news of Jesus Christ with those who do not know him! I would also like to encourage you to read Psalm 107. It is a little too long to include in its entirety in this chapter, but I would like to focus on a few verses that I hope spurn your heart to action:

Some wandered in desert wastes,
finding no way to a city to dwell in;
hungry and thirsty,
their soul fainted within them.
Then they cried to the LORD in their trouble,
and he delivered them from their distress . . .
He sent out his word and healed them,
and delivered them from their destruction.

(Psalm 107:4–6, 20)

6

The Great I AM and the Paper Lion

The day was ramping up to be crazy. There were two autistic kids on our unit who were admitted because they had become so violent at home that their parents could not control them and no longer felt safe. One had been brought to our facility in shackles, and the other had recently been transferred to our unit to give the previous unit a break from his extreme behavior. October tends to be an active month for behavioral health patients, and this month was setting new records. My pager went off. One of my new nurses called me for help. One of the two autistic patients was hitting his family, trying to bite anyone who wasn't quick enough to move out of the way, and yelling every known profanity at the top of his lungs. This would be the third time we called security that day, and it was only nine thirty in the morning. Little did I know how long of a day it would be.

I walked into the room and noted that the patient had inched his way around the room and was focusing most of his aggression toward his nurse. I quickly stepped in to intervene. After reminding him that spitting at people was not appropriate behavior, I had gotten his attention. He lunged at me, and I stepped quickly around a nightstand, trying to put some distance between us. When I asked him to sit on the bed, he looked me dead in the eyes, sneered, and said a very deep voice in third person, "He doesn't want to." I had seen that look before, long ago in a jungle-filled paradise, but this time I was not afraid.

In the past couple of chapters I have alluded to and skirted around the enemy that I will now address. There is this blindness in Western culture that pervades even those who follow Jesus. No one wants to believe, let alone acknowledge the elephant in the room, and it is this: There is God, whom we serve, and there are angels, demons, and Satan. Even as I type these words I feel as though I am losing some of you. I pray it will not be so. May the Lord use me to challenge your understanding of creation and the world in which we live.

In Paul's letter to the Ephesian church, he very clearly says that there is more to this physical world than what meets the eye. He says,

> Finally, be strong in the Lord and in the strength of his might. Put on the whole armor of God, that you may be able to stand against the schemes of the devil. For we do not wrestle against flesh and blood, but against the rulers, against the authorities, against the cosmic powers over this present darkness, against the spiritual forces of evil in the heavenly places. (6:10–12)

You see, there is heaven, hell, and a whole spiritual realm that we cannot see with the naked eye.

Furthermore, in this passage we get the sense that there is a serious conflict surrounding us. The apostle Paul says that we are "wrestling" with unseen forces. These are not small, insignificant beings. The wording used in the passage paints the picture of large forces and a hierarchal system. An army comes to mind. However, before Paul even describes these unseen forces or conflict, he calls the reader to dress themselves in spiritual armor. My friends, the only time armor is *ever* needed is in battle. And with forces so vast, this is not just tension or a "cold war." This is war—war on a large scale, war that many of us are sleepwalking through.

This epic war involves mankind, angels and demons, Satan, and God. This is a battle for God's glory that is the result of the actions of one rebellious, prideful creature. Before we address him or any other player in this cosmic war, though, I want to first and foremost turn our attention to God. If we want to understand anything, we must start with God, the Creator, Savior, and ultimate King. Having a clear understanding of who God is will give us better insight into who we are and who the enemy is. I hope you will see that everything pales in comparison to this all-powerful, mighty, terrible, unique, beautiful, loving God.

The Great I AM, The Lord of Hosts

This may seem like a silly question, but who is God? I ask this crucial question purposefully, because I want you to question your knowledge of God. Do you know who he is? How much time have you spent trying to understand his character? If you doubt who he is or if he is real, is it because of a lack of evidence or because of a lack of searching? And when you search for him, are you looking to find what he can give you, or are you seeking to know him? With these questions in mind, let me give you a little teaser trailer. I cannot possibly dive into all of who God is in this chapter or even in this book, but I hope the next few paragraphs will spark a hunger for more.

Throughout the Bible God calls himself "I AM." And he uses this term as both his name and as a descriptor of who he is. In Isaiah 46:9–10 he says, "I am God, and there is no other; I am God, and there is none like me, declaring the end from the beginning and from ancient times things not yet done." In this brief statement, God is telling us quite a bit about who he is. First, he is telling us that he is God. Then he immediately follows that statement with the information that there isn't a host of gods; there is only one God, I AM. Let me repeat this: *There are no other gods. It is just I AM.* Then, just in case we still are searching for another option, he states that he is unique. Therefore, we learn that there is only one God in existence. We know his name, and he is unique.

The passage also gives us insight into his existence. Verse 10 says that he declares "the end from the beginning and from the ancient times things not yet done." A couple chapters later, in Isaiah 48:12, he says, "I am he; I am the first, and I am the last." You see, if he knows the end from the beginning and he declares the future from ancient times, the laws of time do not apply to him and he is beyond time. This is confirmed in his statement that he is the first and the last. How would you know the beginning and end or the first occurrence and the last unless you have witnessed them? God is not regulated by time as you and I are because he created time and is not bound by his creation. *HE* defines all of creation: "I am the Alpha and the Omega, the first and the last, the beginning and the end" (Revelation 22:13).

Not only is God outside of time, he is eternal. This means he has always been and will always be. There was no moment of conception or spark into being. He is not the product of other, older beings or the outcome of atoms and molecules colliding. He always was. This is a very hard concept to wrap our minds around because we are so very finite, but pause and think on this. There has never been, nor will there ever be, a moment God did not exist. He has always been and will always be present—before time, within time, and after time.

How do we know this? Where is the evidence of such claims? Prophesy throughout God's inspired Word has been fulfilled perfectly, over and over and over, in and through the life of Jesus as well as in the history of the nation of Israel. It all came to pass, not by man's ability or by coincidence, but by God's foreknowledge given to his servants. Over and over, throughout the generations, "The word of the LORD came"[1] to men who, in boldness, declared things that were to come. And they have all come to pass, exactly as they have been foretold.

This shows us that God is omniscient, meaning, "He knows everything: everything possible, everything actual; all events and all creatures, of the past, the present and the future . . . Nothing escapes his notice, nothing can be hidden from him, nothing is forgotten by him."[2] The psalmist gives us insight into this when he says, "Great is our Lord and abundant in strength; His understanding is infinite" (Psalm 147:5 NASB). This is why he is able to address the future from our past. However, his omniscience points to something deeper and more difficult to grasp: that he is eternal. How can God know everything unless he is beyond time? And if he is beyond time, then he must be eternal.

Accordingly, throughout the Bible God makes *everlasting* promises. For example, In Isaiah 45:17, God promises to save Israel with *everlasting* salvation. In Jeremiah 31:3, he promises to love Israel with an *everlasting* love. In Daniel 4:3, his kingdom is described as *everlasting*. And in in Ephesians 1:4, we are told that as Christians, "he chose us in him before the foundation of the world, that we should be holy and blameless before him."

---

[1] Jeremiah 1:4, Zechariah 4:8, Ezekiel 16:1, & many others
[2] Arthur W. Pink, *The Attributes of God*, (Grand Rapids: Baker Books, 2006), 21.

Since we are trying to better understand who God is, who does he say he is? He says he is the Lord.[3] He is the first and the last.[4] He is the *only* God.[5] He is the God of all flesh.[6] He is from above, not of this world.[7] He is our one and only savior.[8] He is the bread of life.[9] He is the good shepherd.[10] He is the one who sanctifies us,[11] who blots out our transgressions for his own sake.[12] He is the one who rebuilds ruined places and replants that which is desolate.[13] He is like a lion[14] and is the door of the sheep.[15] He is Jesus.[16] He is the God of Abraham, and he is with us.[17] He is Holy.[18] He is the performer of his word.[19] He is our help.[20] He is the one who forms light and creates darkness, who makes wellbeing and creates calamity.[21] He is the living one who died and is alive forever more, who has the keys to death and Hades.[22] He is with us always, to the end of the age.[23]

You see, God is the sustenance, fullness, and enjoyment of life. He knows the past and the future and is outside of time. There was none before him, and there will be none after him. He endures. He is constant, sure, and without beginning. He is not defined by anything or anyone else, but he defines and bears witness to himself. He has power and

---

[3] Leviticus 11:45
[4] Isaiah 48:12
[5] Isaiah 46:9
[6] Jeremiah 32:27
[7] John 8:23
[8] Isaiah 43:11
[9] John 6:35
[10] John 10:14
[11] Leviticus 20:8
[12] Isaiah 43:25
[13] Ezekiel 36:36
[14] Hosea 13:7
[15] John 10:7
[16] Acts 26:15
[17] Genesis 26:24
[18] Leviticus 11:44
[19] Jeremiah 1:12
[20] Isaiah 41:13
[21] Isaiah 45:7
[22] Revelation 1:17–18
[23] Matthew 28:20

authority over everything. He is the ruler by preeminence. He is the owner and head of everything. There is no other God, just him, and he is truly unique. He is the ultimate prize, and he fully satisfies with abundance. He is not human, but so much more. He is not of this world, nor is he confined to it. He is the answer to your questions, your searching. He is the one who can and will save; there is no second option. God is present outside our story. He is bigger than it, older than history, and present at the beginning. He is good. God wants to give a full life to his creation. He is in charge, yet he purifies, enables, and restores. He is sovereign and holy, weaving history for his glory. He is a personal king. He is owner and God over all flesh, all humanity and creatures. He is the ruler of all, but he also teaches the individual. He is life-giving and the creator of all. He is triune. He does not abandon his creation; he has a plan. He has the power to clean up your mess, not only for your sake, but for his glory. He rebuilds and restores. He savors and enjoys life and order. He loves beauty and turns ugly things into beautiful things. He is owner, and he keeps his word, always. He fights and works for the good of his creation. He is terrible and mighty; he is gentle and the entrance into a full life. He keeps his promises and is faithful. He does not abandon those whom he chooses. He is a God of words, speech, and action. He is eternal and alive. He is not bound by the same rules we are. Nothing, not even death, has power over God. He controls death and is beyond death's grasp. He is always present and always involved, until he returns, and even then he will still be present!

This is the God of the Bible, the God whom we serve because he called us. Do you feel overwhelmed? I do, and the authors of the Bible were as well. Moses describes God as "a consuming fire" (Deuteronomy 4:24), the "God of gods and Lord of lords, the great, the mighty, and the awesome God" (Deuteronomy 10:17), and "merciful and gracious, slow to anger, and abounding in steadfast love and faithfulness" (Exodus 34:6). The psalmist describes him as "a God of salvation" (Psalm 68:20); gracious, righteous, and merciful[24]; powerful and full of majesty.[25] The prophets saw his might and described God as "the God of hosts" (Hosea 12:5), "an everlasting rock" (Isaiah 26:4), and "a jealous and avenging God" who is in opposition to those who are his enemies, not making deals with them but saving all of his terrible wrath for them (Nahum 1:2).

---

[24] Psalm 116:5
[25] Psalm 29:4

As Christians, it is so easy to get focused on secondary things. We work hard to maintain a façade of a "good Christian." We obsess over Satan's impact in our lives. We strive to be known as prayer warriors and deacons and Bible study teachers. We read more devotionals, watch more sermons, listen to more podcasts, and wear ourselves out trying to self-grow deeper faith. Friends, can I tell you that these things, as wonderful as they are, are secondary? Not a single one of them should have your focus. Your eyes should be fixed on your Creator.

Do not look for the next devotional; look to God's Word. Don't worry over the enemy, because the enemy fades in view of our God, *who will fight for you.* Do you want to be more powerful in your prayer life? Get to know God deeper. Do you want to have the faith of a spiritual giant? Put more effort into knowing God's character. You will never be the person you desire to be without trying to know God on a deeper level. And yet, we somehow believe that if we focus on his blessings or how he changes us or things we can do for him we can become like the apostles. How silly! That would be like me saying that my favorite part of my husband is the opportunities to cook for him, our intimate times together, how he makes me feel, or how he makes me a better person. All of those things are great, but after a while our marriage would crumble because I would be doing nothing to *know him* on a deeper level. This is a very self-centric approach to the relationship, yet this is so often how we approach God. We get so consumed with how he affects us that we miss *him.*

It is only with our eyes fixed unwaveringly on him that we can have faith that moves mountains, pray prayers that miraculously heal, live an abundant life, and be marked by the Holy Spirit. This is how we must view the enemy and his attack—as one looking from the shadow of the Almighty's wing, completely fearless, because all we can see is our Savior and Victor! That being said, there are some key lessons that we must learn about the enemy. They are not to be central lessons; they should elevate and highlight who God is and what he can do!

Satan, the Accuser

I would like to discuss with you who our adversary, the devil, is. He is the reason this mess exists, and there are a lot of misconceptions about who he is and what he can do. Though I am no expert in this area,

God's Word is very clear about Satan, and I will stick to what God has revealed in his Word. In Job 1, Satan is referred to as an adversary or accuser, but how did he come to be in this role of opposition to God?

In Ezekiel 28, we get a glimpse of the beginning. We find here that Satan is not God's evil equivalent but is in fact a created being, an angel. Though not remotely divine, he was unique. He was the "signet of perfection" (v. 12), beautiful, purposefully created for the role of "guardian cherub" (v. 14). He had unique access to God and had special privileges, implying that he was in a position of power and authority.[26] He followed God and was righteous "till unrighteousness was found" in him (v. 15).

What was the unrighteousness? Isaiah 14:13–14 says,

> You said in your heart,
>   "I will ascend to heaven;
> above the stars of God
>   I will set my throne on high;
> I will sit on the mount of assembly
>   in the far reaches of the north;
> I will ascend above the heights of the clouds;
>   I will make myself like the Most High."

You see, somewhere is his existence, Satan took his eyes off of the only, all-powerful, beautiful, incomparable, almighty, righteous, omniscient, omnipresent God and looked down at himself and the things he had done (for God's glory) and liked what he saw. In that first glance away, his self-obsession birthed pride, which grew into arrogance, which matured into rebellion. Satan was a beautiful, perfect creature who took his eyes off God and sought fulfillment in himself.

Going back to Ezekiel 28, I want to highlight a bit of God's character. In verse 15 we see that unrighteousness was found in Satan's heart, but it's not until verse 16, when he *acted* on that unrighteousness, that God punished him by casting him out of heaven. This reveals God's goodness and justness. He did not punish Satan because of the motives of his heart, though they were worthy of punishment. He punished Satan because of the *actions* he chose. Even in the face of rebellion, God is just.

---

[26] Tony Evans, *The Battle is the Lord's* (Chicago: Moody Press, 1998).

Satan is now a shadow of what he once was, because it is God who defines and makes creation beautiful. When the devil was cast out of heaven, he became an example to all of creation. His beauty was stripped, his deeds revealed for all to see, and his might turned to weakness. Though he plays the role of our accuser and acts as our adversary, as Christians we should not look on him as someone to fear but as a lesson to learn from. This is who you are in rebellion and apart from the Lord.

In Isaiah 14:4–21, we see the consequences of the devil's actions. "How the oppressor has ceased, the insolent fury ceased!" verse 4 says. Satan's attempts at power will end, and his oppression of the world and insolence against God will come to an end. God then declares, "The whole world is at rest and quiet; they break forth into singing . . . All of them will answer and say to you: 'You too have become as weak as we! You have become like us!' Your pomp is brought down to Sheol, the sound of your harps; maggots are laid as a bed beneath you, and worms are your covers" (vv. 7, 10–11). Peace has come through Jesus and will be fully completed when he comes again and Satan is thrown into hell! Friends, this is Satan's legacy. He who was once one of the mightiest of created beings, the signet of perfection, has now become as weak as man. He who was once beautiful has now become ugly and revolting.

My friends, I said it before and I will say it again: It is God who defines the individual. It is God who makes him mighty, who fills him with beauty, and who gives him power and authority. Satan looked to himself to define himself. His self-love blinded him from reality, and his arrogance filled him with fury. This is why we neither fear the enemy nor dread his attack. The enemy is no longer mighty. Satan and his demons are on the highway to hell. The gates have opened, and Satan's time is rapidly coming to an end. So, beloved, do not worry or look for spiritual attack, but look to the Lord! *He* will define you. *He* will make you strong. *He* will give you authority over the enemy. And the enemy cannot stand against the servants of the Lord who are fully submitted to their Savior.

Though we do not need to fear the enemy, we should not be naïve to his character and his power. In John 8:44, Jesus gives us insight into the devil's character. Satan hates God's Word, because God's Word is sure and true. He is a murderer and a liar. He is, in fact, the inventor of lying. In John 10:10, Jesus refers to Satan as a thief who comes to kill, steal, and destroy, *but* Jesus brings abundant life. Paul tells us in

Ephesians 2 that Satan is walking in sin and death, a concept that the prophet Isaiah alludes to in Isaiah 14. But notice this: in Ephesians 2:2, Satan is depicted as striving for authority over this world and over mankind. He does this by influencing people to "live in the passions of [their] flesh," which is done by "carrying out the desires of the body and the mind" (v. 3).

How does he convince people to live in such a way? This is where his craftiness comes into play. In both Genesis 3:1–6 and Matthew 4:1–11, we get a front row seat to Satan's working to allure people to take their eyes off God and put them on themselves. In both of these passages we watch Satan twist God's spoken Word to create doubt of God's character. He says to Eve, "Did God actually say, 'You shall not eat of any tree in the garden'?" He twists God's words. What God actually said was, "*You may surely eat of every tree in the garden, but of the tree of the knowledge of good and evil you shall not eat, for in the day that you eat of it you shall surely die*" (Genesis 2:16–17, author's emphasis). Unfortunately, we know what happens next. The seed of doubt had been planted, and Eve did not remember the words of God. We are still feeling the shockwaves of her decision to doubt God and look to herself.

And in Matthew 4, we see Jesus tested with the same craftiness that doomed the first man and woman. In Jesus' time of temptation in the wilderness, Satan tried three times to trick Jesus into doubting God and trusting himself. He did this by twisting scripture, by urging Jesus to look to himself to meet his own needs rather than God and by offering Jesus an easy way out. This time, it was Jesus who prevailed. He did not sin like Adam and Eve.

I highlight these two passages to show you that the enemy plays dirty. He will try to use God's own spoken and written Word to trick you and make you doubt God's Word and his character. This is why we must KNOW God's Word verbatim. General familiarity with Scripture will not stand up to the test. Eve was familiar with the gist of what God had commanded her and Adam, and she failed the test.

The Epic War that has Been Won

Lastly, let's look at Revelation 12:7–11. This passage reveals a vibrant picture of the war that is being waged, what the war is being fought over, and the ultimate outcome of this epic war.

"Now war arose in heaven, Michael and his angels fighting against the dragon. And the dragon and his angels fought back, but he was defeated, and there was no longer any place for them in heaven. And the great dragon was thrown down, that ancient serpent, who is called the devil and Satan, the deceiver of the whole world—he was thrown down to the earth, and his angels were thrown down with him. And I heard a loud voice in heaven, saying, "Now the salvation and the power and the kingdom of our God and the authority of his Christ have come, for the accuser of our brothers has been thrown down, who accuses them day and night before our God. And they have conquered him by the blood of the Lamb and by the word of their testimony, for they loved not their lives even unto death."

First of all, I want to point out to you that in this passage we see all the players. There are the angels who follow God, who are under the command of Michael. Then there is the enemy, the devil and deceiver of the whole world, along with the fallen angels who are under his command. There is a war being fought that started in heaven. It is a war that has arisen in response to Satan's rebellion and rages in defense of God's glory. Mercifully, in verse 8, God tells us the ending. The battle ends and Satan is defeated! His end is sure and rapidly approaching.

We know from Isaiah 14 and Ezekiel 28 that God specifically and intentionally created Satan (then, Lucifer) for a particular purpose. When he rebelled against God and ceased to served him, there was no longer a place for him in heaven. He now had sin in his heart and was therefore incapable of serving a holy God, meaning he no longer fit into God's system. So, Satan was banished to earth with his followers, angels whom we now know as demons.

The enemy is powerful, crafty, and deceiving. He and his demons are always at work against God's glory, and Satan accuses God's people day and night. *But he has been defeated and stripped of his power*, as have his demons. God's glory is being shown brilliantly through the salvation and reconciliation of mankind to God's kingdom as well as through the revealed authority of Jesus Christ. How do we know this? Revelation 12:11 says, "They [God's people] have conquered him [Satan] by the blood of the Lamb and by the word of their testimony." This means that God's glory and authority are revealed by their salvation, hope, trust, dependence, and reconciliation to God through Christ Jesus. God's glory is also revealed through the sharing of the gospel, through which people experience firsthand the Lord God Almighty. It is the change brought by being reconciled to God and the drive to pass on this hope that pushes Christians beyond themselves, even to the point of death, because they love God more than themselves.

You see, this is power—the power of God being exemplified through the reconciliation of broken, evil, weak creatures and completely transforming them into a mighty people who can defeat an immensely stronger enemy. Ponder this. Ponder these verses we have covered. As you do, I hope you will begin to see the enemy in light of the great I AM. Suddenly, the enemy will fade and all you will see is God's power. This mighty adversary, this terrible enemy, is nothing more than a paper lion, with no teeth, no power, only a loud roar. God, in comparison, is brilliantly blinding. It is only with our eyes fixed on the Father that his power and glory will be made manifest in our lives.

Dear friends, awake! The King of the universe is calling you to fight! He has saved you; now take up arms in defense of his glory! The enemy is not what you thought, and the power of the Most High is yours to use if you will fix your eyes unwaveringly on him. I pray that as you gaze on him, on his beauty, brilliance, and might, you would be filled with joy, confidence, and hope.

The Battle is the LORD's

And the Philistine moved forward and came near to David, with his shield-bearer in front of him. And when the Philistine looked and saw David, he disdained him, for he was but a youth, ruddy and handsome in appearance. And the Philistine said to David, "Am I a dog, that you come to me with sticks?" And the Philistine cursed David by his gods. The Philistine said to David, "Come to me, and I will give your flesh to the birds of the air and to the beasts of the field." Then David said to the Philistine, "You come to me with a sword and with a spear and with a javelin, but I come to you in the name of the Lord of hosts, the God of the armies of Israel, whom you have defied. This day the Lord will deliver you into my hand, and I will strike you down and cut off your head. And I will give the dead bodies of the host of the Philistines this day to the birds of the air and to the wild beasts of the earth, that all the earth may know that there is a God in Israel, and that all this assembly may know that the Lord saves not with sword and spear. For the battle is the Lord's, and he will give you into our hand."

1 Samuel 17:41–47

The whole story of David and Goliath has intrigued countless people for generations, but verses 41–47 of 1 Samuel 17 in particular always get my heart racing. The story is not just about an underdog shouting in defiance to a bully. It's not about a young kid from a nowhere town stepping up to the plate when everyone else shrinks away. No, this is a story of a young man who understood who God is and defiantly defended the name of the Lord in the face of ridicule, fierce opposition, and virtually no support. David wasn't fearless because he had practice fighting lions as a shepherd. David was fearless because he had seen God deliver him from the mouth of the lion. He understood whom he was fighting for. Who was this human Philistine in contrast to the Lord Almighty?

David is just one of many who did not hesitate to take up arms and fight to defend the Lord's glory. Many of their names you might recognize, men such as Joshua, Gideon, King Josiah, and Jonathan. Others might be lesser known, such us Othniel, Ehud, and Barak. All of these people did so because their eyes were fixed, beyond their enemy, on the Lord. These men had such a clear vision of God that the circumstances didn't matter. They understood fully that the enemy is nothing compared to the Lord and that nothing is impossible for God.

I would even go so far as to argue that these warriors would have said that it was a joy and privilege to defend the name of the Lord. Paul says as much in 1 Timothy 1:12: "I *thank* him who has given me strength, Christ Jesus our Lord, because he judged me faithful, *appointing me to his service*" (author's emphasis). Paul is not necessarily talking about battle or warfare in this passage, but he is talking about being grateful to serve the Lord in any capacity. It is an echo of the heart of King David, who served the Lord as king and in battle.

Friends, as Christ followers, we are called to defend the name and glory of the Lord. The enemy is working hard to steal God's glory in our hearts, in our marriages, in our families and friendships, in our workplaces, and anywhere else God's glory might be revealed. Let me urge you, because you know whom you serve and now better understand his character, it is time to stand in boldness and be ready to defend the glory of our King! Let us not shy away from the necessary confrontation, because he has appointed both you and me to his service.

Paul urges his mentee, Timothy, to "wage the good warfare" (1 Timothy 1:18). What does Paul mean by that statement? In Ephesians we get a better understanding. Paul tells the Ephesian church,

"Finally, be strong in the Lord and in the strength of his might. Put on the whole armor of God, that you may be able to stand against the schemes of the devil. For we do not wrestle against flesh and blood, but against the rulers, against the authorities, against the cosmic powers over this present darkness, against the spiritual forces of evil in the heavenly places. Therefore take up the whole armor of God, that you may be able to withstand in the evil day, and having done all, to stand firm." (Ephesians 6:10–13)

Paul is pushing Timothy and the church in Ephesus to be faithful in defending the glory of God. Boots on the ground, that means trusting and relying on the Lord. It means looking beyond the hurtful people and ugly circumstances to see the real enemy that is at work in people's hearts. It means withstanding sin and protecting yourself from evil by using the tools God has given us.

Paul is trying to get the Ephesian church to understand that there are deeper spiritual things that are happening beyond their current situation. He is trying to get the church to look past their circumstances to see the cosmic battle that is being fought in the midst of their lives. Notice, however, who does Paul point them to first? God. He is urging them to look to God, to trust and to rely on God.

Like Paul, the apostle Peter also warns the early church to be on guard against our enemy the devil. He says, "Be sober minded; be watchful. Your adversary the devil prowls around like a roaring lion, seeking someone to devour. Resist him, firm in your faith, knowing that the same kinds of suffering are being experienced by your brotherhood throughout the world" (1 Peter 5:8–9). Peter is pressing his brothers and sisters in the faith to wake up and be attentive! He warns them by describing the devil as a lion who is ever on the hunt, looking for someone to devour. You see, the battle for God's glory may have begun before the foundation of the world, but the enemy brought the fight to earth when he tempted Adam and Eve to sin in the garden.[1]

We were created to bring God glory. How better to destroy the glory of God than to destroy God's glory in his creatures? However, both Paul and Peter tell us there is hope! "Resist him [the devil], firm in

---

[1] Tony Evans, The Battle is the Lord's (1998).

your faith," says Peter. Resist the devil by your clear vision of the Lord and assurance of who he is! And Paul says, "be strong in the Lord and in the strength of his might . . . take up the whole armor of God, that you might be able to stand against the schemes of the devil." Beloved, don't be self-reliant, but take up God's armor. The only way to resist the enemy is to be dependent on the Lord, to do things his way, by his standards.

In James 4:1–11, the apostle James describes those he is writing to as double-minded, consumed by and enslaved to their desires and passions. They are never satisfied and always wanting more. They are unfaithful. Why are they this way? They are worldly. Jesus and Paul both describe the devil as "the god of this world" (2 Corinthians 4:4, see also John 12:31). In other words, he is the god of worldliness, and he has worked hard to shape the world to reflect his character and depravity. It's Genesis 3 all over again. We see something beautiful, something to be desired, and Satan whispers into that desire, fanning its flame in our hearts. If our eyes are on our desires and not fixed on the Lord, how will we see that we are being consumed until we are burning alive?

This is the dangerous campaign of the enemy. He preys on our desires to draw our hearts and minds away from our Creator and First Love. We are double-minded and don't even realize it, because the enemy has perfected his attack. (How do you think he got all of those angels, who used to serve God and saw him face-to-face, to rebel and walk away from God?) This is why James says in verse 5, "He yearns jealously over the spirit that he has made to dwell in us." Without even noticing it, we have played the whore by both claiming fidelity to our Savior and giving ourselves over to the things we are chasing. This is strong language, I know, but sometimes strong language is necessary to jolt us to reality.

When we try to play games with God, flirting with the world, we are essentially giving our hearts and minds to the enemy. Though that might never be our intention and our desire might really be for God, chasing the world, walking the line between holiness and worldliness, really is like being a juicy little lamb walking by the lion's den for a bit of a thrill. We all know what will happen to that foolish little lamb. Remember the devil is relentlessly on the hunt, always looking for someone to devour.

What are we to do instead? "Submit yourselves therefore to God. Resist the devil, and he will flee from you," James 4:7 says, for God "gives more grace" (v. 6). Wake up! Look around and *see*. Are you bound in chains, unaware in your sleepy stupor? Submit your double-mindedness, your greedy, passion-filled heart to the Lord, because he is gracious. Remember, he "yearns jealously" for you, so come back to him. *Resist* the devil, his whispers and subtle lies. *See* the attack, the true face of the enemy, and he will flee from you, because then you will be at home, devoted again to the Lord, and who can stand against the Lord?

How do we resist the enemy? 2 Corinthians 10:3–6 says,

> For though we walk in the flesh, we are not waging war according to the flesh. For the weapons of our warfare are not of the flesh but have divine power to destroy strongholds. *We destroy arguments and every lofty opinion raised against the knowledge of God, and take every thought captive to obey Christ, being ready to punish every disobedience, when your obedience is complete.* (Author's emphasis)

Though we live in a physical world and in fleshly, human bodies with reflexes, emotions, and baggage, we are not engaging in battle by tapping into our humanity or our natural responses. Instead, by choosing *not* to engage the enemy on human terms but on God's terms we have the God-given power to destroy strongholds of the enemy, whether personal, individual, communal, or national.

We do this logically and humbly, showing people Jesus by communicating and establishing an accurate understanding of who God is. This means that we must have a truthful, personal understanding of God's person and character. According to this passage, we also should be in the habit of submitting every thought to the Lord. In humility, our speech and thoughts must be trained on him. This means that in every capacity we operate in self-control and with intention—logical humility.

It is a heavy responsibility to defend the name and character of your God with a humble heart. This intentional lifestyle is one that births obedience. This means that when we talk to our friends and patients who battle devastating cancers, horrible diagnoses, or unthinkable tragedies, we don't just give them a Sunday school answer. It's easy to say, "Well, God works everything out for good," or "God will not give you anything you cannot handle," or "God is testing your faith; it will all work out." These responses help no one. There is no life or hope in these answers, because they are not Scripture and do not highlight God's glory. In heartache and darkness we can empathize and glorify the Lord by saying, "This is hard and horrible and I am breaking with you. But the darkness does not change who God is. What was true in the light is still true in the dark. He is good and kind. He cares for your heart, and he weeps with you."[2]

This intentional work of pointing people back to Christ in the midst of their brokenness is your faithful obedience at work. Notice that last phrase at the end of 2 Corinthians 10:6 that says, "when *your* obedience is complete." This phrase indicates that we do not have the authority to speak into someone else's life until our own is in line with God. So the training of our minds by the submission of our thoughts to Christ and the training of our tongues to point people to Christ is the process by which God trains our own wills for obedience. This is counterintuitive to our fleshly bend but necessary if we are to partake in kingdom work. Jesus says, "first take the log out of your own eye, and then you will see clearly to take the speck out of your brother's eye" (Matthew 7:5).

Rather than rebel against God, we are called and held to a standard of obedience. Instead of reacting or responding in a way that is fueled by emotion, we are to logically and intentionally respond by revealing Jesus Christ. Even down to the very thoughts floating through our minds. We are to be characterized by meekness, willing submission to the Father. It may not seem like fighting, but it is this faithful dependence on God that the enemy is powerless against. And it is God revealed through this faithful dependence that brings light into the darkness and lasting change into our lives, communities, and nations.

Remember, God is good. Having commanded us to resist the enemy, he has given us the tools to be able to resist him! They are not tools that you and I would consider to be so, but we will explore next how each one of them are to be used to stand firm in the Lord, though the enemy attack us. These tools are spiritual and include prayer, fasting, scripture memory, songs of worship, and the Holy Spirit, who is our Helper.

---

[2] Rend Collective, "Weep With Me," *Good News* (2018).

8

Tools of the Trade

Being a nurse, I often refer to myself as McGyver. Much like the television character from the Eighties, I can come up with a do-it-yourself fix to almost any problem thrown at me. All I need is a rubber band, some gum, and a toothpick. Though my profession has taught me to be resourceful, my God does not demand so much from me. Thank goodness we serve a God who equips us for the task at hand, whether it is fighting or building! The story of Israel's rebuilding the wall of Jerusalem in the book of Nehemiah is such a perfect picture of how we are to tackle the work before us while engaging in battle against our relentless enemy.

Nehemiah opens in the period time when the exiles of Israel had just returned to the rubble of Jerusalem. In chapters 1–2, Nehemiah is granted authority to rebuild the wall around the city. In chapter 4, verse 6, Nehemiah tells us, "the people had a mind to work." In other words, they worked to rebuild the wall with all their hearts. Their fervor, however, did not mean that there would not be difficulty or opposition. While the Israelites where attempting to rebuild the wall, three different people groups came together to attack those who were rebuilding the wall of Jerusalem. In the end it was God who fought for the remnant of Israel. He frustrated the plans of those who opposed the rebuilding of the wall.

Nehemiah's response to the news of this imminent attack was first to pray to God and second to set a guard day and night.[1] He then equipped those working with weapons to defend themselves and their families. Then they all went back to work rebuilding the wall. However, the looming risk of attack changed their way of working. With one hand they worked and with the other they held their weapon.[2] What a picture! Can you imagine it? Men and women were laboring under the sun with their tool for rebuilding in one hand and their weapon of defense in the other.

This is metaphorically what we are to be doing! We are to be working to build the kingdom of God while simultaneously readying ourselves to fight! God has not abandoned us to a lurking enemy; he is actively working to thwart the plans of the enemy. But though God is our defense and the battle is his, it would be foolish for us to not prepare to defend ourselves. In order to do so, God has given us the weapons and tools necessary to complete the task at hand. Prayer, fasting, worship in song, scripture memory, and reliance on the Holy Spirit are all tools that God has given us to be able to complete the task he has called us to. Let's take a look at each of these spiritual tools of the trade.

Prayer

Jesus is the perfect picture of a powerful life submitted to God. Satan could not thwart God's will for Jesus, though he tried very hard to do so. On numerous occasions throughout the Gospels, Jesus would go away from the crowds and pray, or go up to a mountain alone and pray. Communication with God was so important to Jesus that he taught his disciples how to pray in Matthew 6. What fills your conversations with God is a pretty good indicator of what is most important to you, and this prayer in Matthew that we know as the Lord's Prayer shows us how to give up our own agendas in submission to God's. You see, by praying this way we acknowledge and remember God's ultimate authority and our need to submit our will to his. It is only when we do so that our hearts are in a place to be dependent on God.

We need to be a people of prayer. Whether in times of need or plenty we should be crying out to our Father in heaven because he loves

[1] Nehemiah 4:9
[2] Nehemiah 4:17

us deeply and cares for each of us personally. Let's walk through the Lord's Prayer in Matthew 6 together.

Jesus starts the prayer by saying, "Our Father in heaven, hallowed be your name" (v. 9). By beginning the prayer in this way, he is showing us that as we come to the Lord in prayer, we should declare his holiness and treat his name with reverence, as King David did. In Psalm 115:1 David says, "Not to us, O LORD, not to us, but to your name give glory, for the sake of your steadfast love and faithfulness." This declaration of God's holy name comes from a humble heart that is more concerned with honoring and glorifying God's name than its own.

As Jesus continues with the prayer, he says, "Your kingdom come, your will be done, on earth as it is in heaven" (v. 10). This indicates to us that we should be asking God to continue establishing his kingdom here on earth. By doing so, we express our submission to his dominion and authority as Lord and King. Friends, we should have an eager expectancy of God's kingdom being fully realized! We should long for and desire it! Notice that this expression is also a statement. The kingdom of heaven *will* come to earth and God's plan *will* be accomplished in its fullness here on earth, just as it is in heaven. Therefore, as his saints, we should be submitting to God, because he is sovereign and his plan is best.

When we are trusting God's plan and are surrendered to his will being accomplished in the world and in our lives, the resulting overflow is believing that God will sustain and satisfy you. Jesus then says, "Give us this day our daily bread" (v. 11). It is a request for God to sustain you for today and implies a complete trust in God for tomorrow because he has already sustained you every day thus far. This statement also reveals the character of the individual. The person who prays this way is not driven by their appetite but finds satisfaction in God's provision.

The next part of the prayer is, "and forgive our debts, as we also have forgiven our debtors" (v. 12). Beloved, bring your sin to the feet of the Lord in repentance. We must be crying out to God, "Forgive my sins, cover what I owe, because I, myself, cannot pay the cost of my sins." Then, through his forgiveness, feel his grace abound! This is why we can bring him our offenses, because he forgives! Therefore, because we have been forgiven, let us in turn forgive. We should mirror the grace and mercy that has been bestowed on us. Grace, forgiveness, and reconciliation should all be sought, even in secret before the Lord, because Jesus, through grace and forgiveness, reconciled you to the Father.

Jesus ends the prayer saying, "And lead us not into temptation, but deliver us from evil" (v. 13). This seems like such an ironic request, since two chapters prior to this prayer "Jesus was led up by the Spirit into the wilderness to be tempted by the devil" (4:1). What I think Jesus is teaching us is that it is okay to ask the Lord to spare us from seasons of temptation and testing, because we know our spiritual weakness. The apostle James helps us to understand this temptation better when he says, "Let no one say when he is tempted, 'I am being tempted by God,' for God cannot be tempted with evil, and he himself tempts no one. But each person is tempted when he is lured and enticed by his own desire" (James 1:13–14). Therefore, ask the Lord to deliver you from evil! Ask the Lord to root out the evil in your heart and to deliver you from the snare of the enemy. Ask the Lord to save you before you even see the enemy, because you are powerless without the Lord.

In Acts 4, we see the early church actually live out this prayer. Peter and John had just been released from prison and were forbidden to talk about Jesus any more. They immediately went back to the rest of the believers and told them everything that had just happened. Their unified response was to pray and seek the Lord. As they prayed they quoted Psalm 2:1–2, which is a psalm of David that accurately prophesied Israel's and the world's rejection of Jesus. By praying this scripture, they were saying that they understood that Jesus' rejection was foreknown by God, that his suffering and death were planned and expected from the beginning. In other words, Jesus' suffering and death was not a surprise to God. Through the course of the prayer, they essentially declared trust in God for their futures, making the connection that if Jesus' suffering was foreknown and planned, so was theirs.

However, this is the incredible part! Rather than ask God to take away their persecution and rejection by man, they asked for BOLDNESS to accomplish God's will! God's will is to reconcile all people to himself through salvation in Jesus Christ, often through healing and miracles. Their prayer was a reflection of their Christ-like meekness. It revealed a submission to God's will and dependence on him to act according to his plan. Look at these early believers and learn from them! We can be confident in this: nothing is a surprise to God! This allows you to trust God to sustain you, fill you with heavenly boldness, provide for others, miraculously reveal Christ, and accomplish the impossible for his glory.

In Mark 9 we see that Jesus does accomplish the impossible. He delivers a boy from a demon who has oppressed him for years. This particular demon caused seizures that almost killed the boy on multiple occasions. Though Jesus' disciples tried to cast out the demon, they were unable to. It was not until Jesus came and sent the demon out with authority that it left. Jesus rebuked the demon and broke the spiritual bondage of the boy, reviving him and saving him from a hopeless situation. Later Jesus' disciples come to him and ask why they were unable to cast out the demon, and he tells them, "This kind cannot be driven out by anything but prayer" (v. 29).

You see, Jesus lived the prayer he modeled in Matthew 6. He was working to establish God's kingdom on earth, under the Father's authority, submitted to his plan, teaching and demonstrating how to be a part of that kingdom. The evidence we see of God's kingdom being realized here on earth is by the breaking the stronghold of the enemy one life at a time. He was not concerned with his own glory but God's, because he was submitted to the will of the Father. Therefore, Jesus was acting under the authority of God and had power over the impossible and authority over the most resilient enemy. It was in this teaching moment that Jesus taught his disciples who they were up against and who's authority they were to operate in; not their own, but the Father's.

This is why we must learn to pray like Jesus—fully submitted to God and his will, completely dependent on him. Like the disciples, we often try to overstep into territory where we have no power or authority. God's power in man does not come because we know all the answers, because we follow God, or even because we are his children. No, when we seek the Lord in prayer, he gives us power and authority because our agendas fade as our hearts align humbly with his agenda, enabling us to perform his will.

Maybe this is why we are often powerless when faced with the enemy. Perhaps our agendas and wills are not submitted to God's will because we value our plans and comfort over the advancement of the kingdom of God. How are you praying? Are your prayers filled with your agenda, comfort, hopes, and plans? Or are they seeking God's?

Fasting

Another powerful tool that we have in our arsenal that is often overlooked is fasting. Too often we forget the practice of fasting and completely miss the God-given, God-dependent power that can only come through fasting. Many of us see fasting as optional, but when Jesus discussed fasting with his disciples in Matthew chapter 6, he said, "And when you fast . . ." (v. 16). He did not say "*if* you fast" but "*when*." This implies an expectation that fasting be a normal and routine discipline of the person who follows Christ.

So what is fasting? And why is it necessary? The first time we see fasting in the Bible is in Judges 20:26, which is in the wake of unspeakable, nauseating evil committed by one of the tribes of Israel. In response to the grievous sin committed, the whole nation rose up and confronted the tribe of Benjamin with the purpose of purging the evil from the people. The tribe of Benjamin, however, was unrepentant and callous to the sin committed, and so a battle ensued. After two devastating losses, the people (both civilians and the army) united, grieved by the sin and devastating loss of life. Together they "came to Bethel and wept. They sat there before the LORD and fasted that day until evening, and offered burnt offerings and peace offerings before the LORD." Then they went up a third time into battle and the Lord delivered the tribe of Benjamin into their hand. Did you catch it? It was when they *fasted* before the Lord that he gave them victory.

This was not an attempt to manipulate God, but an expressed dependency on him and a humbling of heart. It is good to seek the Lord, but to be utterly dependent on the Almighty in acknowledgement of your finite place before an infinitely holy God is a game changer. How can we expect to resist the spiritual forces of evil in this present darkness if we are not dependent on the Lord? 1 Corinthians 1:27–29 says, "God chose what is weak in the world to shame the strong; God chose what is low and despised in the world, even things that are not, to bring to nothing things that are, so that no human being might boast in the presence of God." God can use us in powerful ways, but we must be completely dependent on him. This kind of dependency is expressed in the discipline of fasting.

The first instance of individual fasting recorded in the Bible was carried out by King David. David stands apart from so many others in Scripture because of his wholehearted devotion to the Lord. God used David (and still does!) to show his people what wholehearted devotion to him looks like. This is exemplified, in part, through fasting. Prior to this point in the Bible,[3] we see the nation of Israel fast under a leader's direction, when seeking victory over an enemy or when begging for deliverance from an enemy. Rarely is it voluntary. Then King David

---

[3] 2 Samuel 1:12

comes along and fasts on his own, repeatedly, and not under coercion but of his own volition. Yes, he is seeking deliverance from his enemies at times and victory at other times, but he seeks the Lord consistently and repeatedly and becomes more and more dependent on God through fasting.

In the New Testament, we see a new face of fasting. Acts 13:2–3 records the early church fasting in worship, out of the joy of communing with the Lord. Note that it is not until the New Testament, after the Holy Spirit has been poured out on God's people, that fasting is seen as a joyful act of worship. When our hearts are right before God and fully submitted to his will, fasting becomes a joyful overflow of devotion. Dependency on God is a beautiful thing that is rooted in joy! Through redemption and sanctification in Jesus Christ our cry through fasting becomes, "Make me more dependent on you, O Lord!"

Sing to the Lord a New Song

It is virtually impossible to read a portion of the Bible and not encounter a song. The Bible is filled with people singing songs. Though there are many songs of mourning, there are even more songs of praise to God. In Psalm 150, every living thing is commanded to praise God. In fact, all of creation does, even if we are unaware of it. The wild animals honor God because he provides for them.[4] The mountains and hills break forth into singing, and the trees clap their hands in worship.[5] The birds sing their morning melodies to their Creator, the oceans roar, and the fields exult![6] From the least to the greatest, creation sings praises to God. I do not think we truly understand how significant this is! If all of creation is praising God, we too must join in the chorus!

Beloved, there are many reasons to praise the Lord, but we should always praise him for his awesome works! In Exodus 15, we see the first recorded song of the Bible. It is also the first recorded time that the people of God respond to his works in a song of praise. Just before this, in 14:31, "Israel saw the great power that the LORD used against the Egyptians, so the people feared the LORD, and they believed the

---

[4] Isaiah 43:20
[5] Isaiah 55:12
[6] 1 Chronicles 16:32

LORD and in his servant Moses." Then the very next sentence, 15:1, says, "Then Moses and the people of Israel sang this song to the LORD."

The nation of Israel had just witnessed with their very own eyes the ten plagues wreak havoc on the nation of Egypt and God part the Red Sea for their escape. They also witnessed Pharaoh's personal demise as well as his military's decimation. They had *seen* God guide them as a pillar of smoke by day and a pillar of fire by night. And. He. Saved. Them. Their response was an overflow of emotion. They understood God's power, by which they had been rescued, so a song of praise burst forth from their mouths.

In the Bible we also encounter people singing in triumph and joy because the Lord fights victoriously for his people! The fall of the city of Jericho was such a circumstance. The nation was commanded, "Shout, for the LORD has given you the city" (Joshua 6:16) Commentator Matthew Henry says,

> This was a triumphant shout, a shout of prayer and an echo of the sound of the trumpets which declared the promise that God would remember them. And at the end of time, when our LORD descends from heaven with a shout and the sound of a trumpet, Satan's kingdom will be completely torn down. But the victory will not be compete until then, when all opposition and every principality and power will be eternally destroyed.[7]

The people of Israel shouted in jubilant expectancy as they waited for the Lord to deliver their enemy into their hand.

Then, in 2 Chronicles 20, there is the incredible account of the nation of Judah going into battle singing. The Israelites were in a desperate situation. A multitude of enemies had come together to destroy the small nation. In response, they fasted and prayed. Then as a nation they came together to seek favor from the Lord. The Lord responded to their cry by saying, "'You will not need to fight in this battle. Stand firm, hold your position, and see the salvation of the LORD on your behalf, O Judah and Jerusalem.' Do not be afraid and do not be dismayed. Tomorrow go out against them, and the LORD will be with you" (v. 17).

---

[7] Matthew Henry. The Matthew Henry Commentary: The Classic Work with Updated Language (Grand Rapids: Zondervan, 2010).

They *believed* the Lord and worshipped him for the salvation *that was coming*. Their leaders addressed them the next morning and reminded them, "Believe in the LORD your God, and you will be established; believe his prophets, and you will succeed" (v. 20). And together they went into battle singing praises to God. As they stood singing, the Lord destroyed their enemies in front of them.

My friends, there is POWER when we sing our praises to God. There is power over the most impossible enemy when we lift up our praises to God in the face of battle. Because when we sing praises to our God and King, our eyes are no longer on our meager strengths and humble resources. Our eyes are not turned inward in pride, nor are our hearts filled with arrogance. When we sing praises to God our eyes are on our Maker, rendering us dependent on him as our hearts turn in submission to him. That is why there is power in singing, because God's power can be fully displayed after we have rightfully been removed from the equation.

In 1 Samuel 16, we get a zoomed-in view of how our spiritual enemy responds to praises sung to the Lord. For a little background, in chapter 12 of 1 Samuel we find out that the Spirit of God had departed from Saul because Saul did not really listen and submit to the Lord. Saul had his own agenda and was not willing to give it up. He had a rebellious heart, and in arrogance he presumed to dictate how he would serve God. Outwardly he appeared to follow God, but inwardly Saul would follow his own way. Therefore, God rejected Saul as king, and the Spirit of God left Saul. God was essentially communicating to him, "Okay, so you want to go your own way? You want to answer to only you? I will give you what you want, and I will leave you."

This is terrifying. God gives Saul what he wants, which leaves a vacancy. What filled the vacancy of the Spirit of God? A demon. Without the protection of the Father by the Holy Spirit's activity in his heart and life, Saul became prey to a demon. This demon was allowed by the Lord to torment and oppress Saul.[8] He was "as if possessed by the devil; by whom he was almost suffocated and strangled, as well as distracted in his counsels, and became weak and foolish; lost all courage and greatness of mind, was timorous and fearful and alarmed by everything, as was full of envy, suspicion, rage and despair."[9] This is what life is like when the umbrella of the Almighty has been removed.

---

[8] 1 Samuel 16:14–15

[9] Matthew Henry, The Matthew Henry Commentary (2010).

Verse 23 of chapter 16 says that "whenever the harmful spirit from God was upon Saul, David took the lyre and played it with his hand. So Saul was refreshed and was well, and the harmful spirit departed from him." Songs of praise to God, the music of praise that overflowed from God's anointed, drove away evil and brought healing and restoration. This is the power of God at work in song.[10]

Finally, I want to point to an incredible story in Acts 17 of the apostles singing praises to God while imprisoned. After being beaten and stoned for sharing the good news of Jesus Christ, Paul and Silas were thrown into prison. That night, bruised and bloody, they prayed together and sang songs of praise to the Lord. While they were singing, the other prisoners were listening. In the middle of their time of worship, God moved in power. A massive earthquake struck in such a way that all the doors to the prison cells were opened. Rather than responding out of self-preservation and fleeing, both apostles stayed and waited for God's leading. In faith they stayed, which eventually led to the salvation of the jailer and his family.

That is the power of God, not only the earthquake, but that through prayer, singing, and a moment-by-moment following of the Lord a man and his whole family came to the saving grace of Jesus Christ. The power of the enemy over them was broken, God was glorified, and his glory was revealed for all to see. When the Lord accomplishes his will, it is a powerful thing, and he invites you into the chorus that you may see firsthand his majesty.

Scripture Memory

In Psalm 119, King David asks, "How can a young man keep his way pure?" In other words, how can someone resist the enemy at work in their life? David answers himself: "By guarding it according to your word. With my whole heart I seek you; let me not wander from your commandments! I have stored up your word in my heart, that I might not sin against you" (vv. 9–11). King David was tuned in to a mystery that we often miss. He understood that to remain pure, to resist the enemy, he had to guard his heart with God's Word. He didn't just

---

[10] Matt Chandler, "The Power of Song," *TVC Resources* (The Village Church, 2018).

recognize God's commands; he was desperate for God's Word. He couldn't get enough of it.

This idea of "storing up" should bring to mind imagery of stockpiling or hoarding. David was not easily satisfied with just reading God's Word. He wanted to accumulate knowledge of it. He intimately knew God's standard for living and used this knowledge to mold his life in a way that pleased God.

Jesus' temptation in the wilderness in Matthew 4 further examines this concept. Satan tempted Jesus to sin, to no avail, by enticing him to do things his own way. First, he tempted Jesus to provide for himself, appealing to Jesus' humanity. He played on that lie that physical needs trump everything. Jesus responded by quoting Deuteronomy 8:3, which says, "Man shall not live on bread alone, but man lives by every word that comes from the mouth of the LORD." His knowledge of Scripture told him it was God who sustained and he could trust God to sustain him. Jesus refused to give in to temptation of going his own way and allowing his flesh to rule him. He declared that he would wait for God and ultimately follow God's way.

Satan then proceeded to tempt Jesus to manipulate God by forcing God's hand. Satan did this by partially quoting Psalm 91:11–12, twisting the words of Scripture to accomplish his own purposes. This should terrify you! The enemy knows God's Word and will twist it to tempt you to sin. He did it with Jesus, he did it with Adam and Eve, and he will do it with you. Do you know Scripture well enough to detect the enemy's twisting of it? Do you know Scripture word for word?

Knowing God's Word—*really knowing* it, hiding it in your heart—can only happen through humble submission to God. This was Jesus' posture. His response to Satan the second time was, "Again it is written, 'You shall not put the Lord your God to the test.'" Essentially he is saying, "I will not presume to make God bow to me, but I will bow in submission to him."

Satan tries one more time to tempt Jesus to sin. He does this by giving Jesus an easy out, with a catch, of course. Satan promises to hand over all the kingdoms of the world, if Jesus would just worship him. No suffering, no cross, an easy transaction. And again Jesus responds with God's Word. He says, "Be gone, Satan! For it is written, 'You shall worship the Lord your God and him only shall you serve.'" Ultimately,

Jesus tells Satan to leave, because he will serve no one and nothing besides God Almighty.[11]

I share this passage with you to show you that Jesus knew Scripture and used it to resist the enemy. He shows us by example the depths to which we are to know Scripture and how we are to use it to remain holy before our holy God. We must know God's Word if we are to know who God is, who the enemy is, and who we are. God's Word reminds us that God is good and faithful, even when we are not. It teaches us that he will sustain us, even when we are weak and powerless. We must move beyond reading the Bible to meditating on it and memorizing it. How will we remember these things in times of testing if we cannot remember them in times of ease?

The apostle Peter alludes to this when he says, "Since therefore Christ suffered in the flesh, arm yourselves with the same way of thinking" (1 Peter 4:1). This is an interesting sentence filled with deep truth. The phrase "arm yourselves" leads me to Ephesians 6, where Paul talks about putting on God's armor. Both passages imply a preparation for war. A hothead doesn't put on protection for a fight, but a soldier does. The hothead responds to one person. He reacts. The soldier prepares to fight an army.

Here is another interesting point. In verse 17 of Ephesians 6, Paul tells the Ephesian church to "take the helmet of salvation." Why is it salvation that guards our minds? Why not, for instance, righteousness? We equip righteousness as a breastplate because our hearts are bent on evil.[12] Righteousness guards the motives of our hearts. Our minds, though, need something else; they can be tricky. It is the thoughts of our minds, fueled by the motives of our hearts, that turn people away from God. But why does salvation play the key role in guarding out minds? Because it is necessary to know and remember who we are and who our Savior is. Remember! We are nothing compared to God, and we are so very weak. Remember that we were clothed in death, drowning in sin, and headed for destruction. In rage and bitterness we faced the world. This is the ugliness that HE, Jesus Christ, saved you from! Jesus, your hope and Savior, suffered for you to give you life and to rescue and ransom you from sin and death. He suffered knowing the cost, confident in the Father's plan. Therefore, arm yourself, prepare yourself with this same way of thinking, so that when you suffer and are tempted you can

---

[11] Matthew 4:1–10
[12] Matthew 15:18–20

be confident in Jesus and his plan. You have already tasted and seen that he is good.

This preparation of our minds, which is accomplished through meditation on and memorization of God's Word, should change our way of thinking. We might be bound to our earthly bodies,[13] but we are no longer to be controlled by our human passions, physical needs, or hearts' motives. By training our minds, we become passionate about and driven to live for God's will. You see, God changes the motives of our hearts, but we choose with our minds what we will do with those motives. This is why we need to immerse ourselves in God's Word and have a full, accurate knowledge of it.

In John 8, Jesus tells the Jews who believed in him, "If you abide in my word, you are truly my disciples, and you will know the truth, and the truth will set you free" (vv. 31–32). Beloved, don't just read God's Word; hoard it, memorize it, soak in it. Dig deeper and deeper and deeper. His words, the Bible, are words of life! Cling to them and watch them empower and change you.

The Holy Spirit

There is this idea that pervades humanity that "where there is a will, there is a way." We think, if I work hard enough, or train long enough, or learn in depth enough, I will prevail. However, as we have seen in Scripture and through the course of this book, this way of thinking is contrary to God's truth. Every single book of the Bible talks about the weakness of mankind, whether in relation to sin, an enemy, our physical bodies, or our spiritual fervor. The Old Testament in particular gives us account after account of men who, in their pride, believed they were strong only to find at their moment of ruin that they were not.

Nowhere in the God's Word is spiritual weakness highlighted more than in the scattering of the disciples when Jesus was arrested. Jesus' hour finally had come and the Jewish religious leaders had come to arrest him. After a few brief moments of tension, Jesus was arrested and his disciples ran away. Mark, the author of the gospel that bears his name, says of Jesus' followers and closest friends, "And they all left him and fled" (14:50). These men had followed Jesus for years. They had

---

[13] 1 Peter 4:2

seen him cast out demons, teach with God's authority, walk on water, and rebuke the raging storm with his spoken word. They had seen him heal people in impossible ways and raise people from the dead and had met the people whose lives he changed. They'd even confessed that he was the Messiah! You cannot get better training or be more prepared than these men. Yet, now we see these men run away, and Peter goes so far as to deny *three times* that he knows Jesus!

Beloved. We. Are. Weak. Our humanity is *not* enough, but Jesus knows this! Right before this whole series of events happened, Jesus warned his disciples, "Watch and pray that you may not enter into temptation. The spirit indeed is willing, but the flesh is weak" (Mark 14:38). Jesus knows our weakness, and in his grace, Jesus sent us God's Holy Spirit to help and guide us.

In the Gospel of John, Jesus tells his disciples, "If you love me, you will keep my commandments. And I will ask the Father, and He will give you another Helper, to be with you forever" (14:15–16). The way Jesus says this implies that it is a known fact that if you love Jesus you will live by his standard. His promise is that he will give the Holy Spirit to those who love him. And the Holy Spirit will help those who love Jesus to keep God's commandments.

In these short couple of verses we learn a few things about the Holy Spirit. We learn that He is called Helper, which can also be translated to "Advocate" or "Counselor." According to Merriam-Webster, a helper is one who assists.[14] Webster also defines *advocate* as "one who pleads the cause of another" or "promotes the interests of a cause or group" (i.e. the Church or the kingdom of God).[15] Finally, Webster defines *counselor* as someone who gives advice.[16] This includes advice regarding God's law.

Another thing we learn about the Holy Spirit is that when he comes, he will come to us forever. This is not a limited-time offer or a lease agreement. This is a lasting and eternal gift, and it is a gift that was promised to God's people generations before Jesus mentioned it. In Isaiah 59:21, the prophet Isaiah relays God's promise:

---

[14] "helper." *Merriam-Webster.com*. 2019. https://www.merriam-webster.com (2 Mar 2019).

[15] "advocate." *Merriam-Webster.com*. 2019. https://www.merriam-webster.com (2 Mar 2019).

[16] "counselor." *Merriam-Webster.com*. 2019. https://www.merriam-webster.com (2 Mar 2019).

"as for me, this is my covenant with them," says the LORD: "My Spirit that is upon you, and my words that I have put in your mouth, shall not depart out of your mouth, or out of the mouth of your offspring, or out of the mouth of your children's offspring," says the LORD, "form this time forth and forevermore."

This promise, made hundreds of years before it came to pass, was reinforced by Jesus' promise to his disciples. Through the prophet Isaiah, God promised that his Spirit would be "upon" his people and that when it happened it would be forever.

Jesus goes on to explain what the Holy Spirit will do when he comes. In John 16, he tells us that the Spirit of God will prove to the world their guilt in relation to sin, their lack of righteousness, and their just and eminent judgment. Jesus then tells his disciples that the Holy · Spirit will do this by proving to the world that their sin is rooted in their rejection of Jesus, which reveals their rebellion against God. He will also prove to the world that Jesus *is* the righteous standard because he comes from God and is in right standing before God, as evidenced by his ascension into heaven[17] and his placement of honor at the right hand of God.[18] Finally, he will prove to the world that their judgment is just and it is coming. And he will do this by revealing Satan for who he is, a rebellious creature who has been judged. Those who follow Satan will have the same outcome as him.

Jesus also reveals to his disciples that the Holy Spirit will guide those who follow and love him into all truth. Notice, *he* will lead God's people to truth. This is a promise and a hope we can rest in. The Holy Spirit will speak under God's ultimate authority and will glorify Jesus. He will also be our direct line to God, through Jesus Christ. Friends, these promises should fill you with hope and peace! It doesn't matter that we are weak, because as followers of Jesus Christ, we have a Helper, who is our Advocate, who is God's Spirit, full of the power of God to change hearts!

The even better news is that this promise, which echoed through the centuries, has been fulfilled! In Acts 2, we have this beautiful scene of the Holy Spirit being poured out on the early Christians. The writer

---

[17] Luke 24:51
[18] Acts 7:55

says, "And they were all *filled* with the Holy Spirit" (v. 4). Again in Acts 10:44 we again see the Holy Spirit "fall" on those who had come to believe in Jesus. If you believe in Jesus and have chosen to follow him, the Holy Spirit has been given to you too! Are you using this resource? Have you let the Spirit of God guide you and help you and counsel you in the way of the Lord?

Dear friends, the battle is the Lord's, but he has called us to wake up and fight for the glory of his name as we fiercely push back the darkness. He is good and has given us many tools for battle. Now that we have understanding of the spiritual weapons God has given us to push back the darkness with, let me encourage you through the words of our Savior:

> I saw Satan fall like lightning from heaven. Behold I have given you authority to tread on serpents and scorpions, and over all the power of the enemy, and nothing shall hurt you. *Nevertheless, do no rejoice in this, that the spirits are subject to you, but rejoice that your names are written in heaven.* (Luke 10:18–20)

9

A Changed Perspective

I will never forget the first time I met my husband. I had just begun my freshman year of college and I had only been in the US for a couple of months. It was nice to start with a clean slate, to begin a completely new chapter, knowing absolutely no one. I loved meeting new people and tried to get involved with as much as I could. The Baptist Student Ministry at my university quickly became home, and I spent many hours in that building making friends, eating free food, and building memories.

I had decided, with a couple other girls, to join the weekly Bible study offered and sheepishly walked into an old, mildew-smelling room, full of old couches. Little did I know that those people in that room would become dear and lifelong friends. Nervously, I tucked my long, straightened hair behind my ear and scanned the room. My eyes stopped on a relatively good-looking guy across the room. I could not help but stare aghast at him. He was reclined on his left side, taking up the majority of the couch with his right leg resting on the top back of the couch. His completely relaxed and nonchalant state left me utterly flabbergasted and confused. Culture shock was hitting. For a girl who grew up in Southeast Asia, this posture for a Bible study was completely inappropriate and rude. Lets just say, I was anything BUT attracted to him on that day.

After the Bible study, he came over to talk to a couple others and myself. I couldn't help but laugh at him. However he chose to sit, he was actually a pretty funny guy . . . but what was his name again? Through the course of the semester I kept running into him, through mutual friends, at the cafeteria, in Bible study, and in the library. I would see him at late-night volleyball games and driving down the street. We became fast friends, and one night my perspective changed. I found myself wondering if he cared that I was going to a baseball game with another guy, or if he wanted to go to Taco Bell for a late night-snack. I started to notice how attractive he was and how he was so skilled at playing the guitar. He had such a way with people, and everyone seemed to know and like him.

Eventually he asked me on a first date that turned out to be a total disaster. I'm still not sure why I went on a second date with him, but I am so glad that I did! Almost thirteen years in and I am floored by the gift that he is. He is what every woman wants in a husband and what every child needs in a father. He loves deeply, and every day with him is an adventure.

I could go on and on about this godly man that is my husband, but I give you a peek into our story to make this point: if my perspective of him had not changed I would have missed out on a deep love, my best friend, and one of the greatest treasures I have ever known. Beloved, if we do not change our perspectives of our careers and those we encounter on a daily basis, we will miss out on a beautiful journey and some priceless treasure that God has in store for us.

Loved and Loving as the Beloved

How we view others is directly related to how we view God and how well we understand our relationship with him. Do you realize that you are loved, deeply loved, by God? He loves you with the fierceness of a Father and the tenderness of a husband. And his love for you is revealed in Jesus Christ. If God's love for us is revealed through Christ, let us first look at how much God loves Jesus.

Throughout the Gospels, God refers to Jesus as "the Beloved" or "my beloved Son." *Beloved* means "dearly loved; dear to the heart."[1] Thus, Jesus is exceedingly loved by God and is cherished by God's

---

[1] "beloved." *Merriam-Webster.com.* 2019. https://www.merriam-webster.com (2 Mar 2019).

heart. These are deep, emotive words that reflect a beautiful relationship filled with love. John the Baptist testified to this loving relationship when he told his disciples, "The Father *loves* the Son and has given all things into his hand" (John 3:35, author's emphasis). This love is unrestricted and deep. God holds nothing back from his beloved Son.

A couple of chapters later, in John 5:20–21, Jesus himself describes God's love for him, saying, "For the Father *loves* the Son and shows him all that he himself is doing. And greater works than these will he show him, so that you may marvel. For as the Father raises the dead and gives them life, so also the Son gives life to whom he will." Just as we saw that God, in love, does not withhold anything from Jesus, we see here that Jesus is even privy to God's plans and working. However, notice that it is not just for Jesus' sake that God displays his love in such a way, but for our sake as well. The Father loves the Son and reveals his plan to love the world through the Son, and the Son loves the Father and submits to the Father's will.

It's a beautiful picture—unencumbered love fully displayed and reciprocated between the Father and the Son that we now see overflows to us. This deep relationship shows that the Father and Son are united; they are one. Everything that Jesus does is only in tandem with, in accordance to, what God the Father is doing. His will is the Father's will because he loves the Father. God desires to bring the dead back to life; therefore, that is also Jesus' desire. This is why Jesus came to raise the dead to life.

In John 11:25–26, Jesus declares, "I am the resurrection and the life. Whoever believes in me, though he die, yet shall he live, and everyone who lives and believes in me shall never die." In this statement, Jesus is again revealing that he is God and is one with the Father by referencing himself with God's name, "I Am." He also reveals that he is carrying out God's will. Once more we are shown that God's will is to bring people back from the dead and give life. God deeply loves Jesus, and they are united in love and will.

God loves his creation, specifically this world, and uses his Son to demonstrate his love for us. Now, in John 3:16, Jesus tells us that "God so loved the world, that he gave his only Son, that whoever believes in him should not perish but have eternal life." By the death of the beloved Son, we who were once dead may be raised to life. As the apostle Paul says is Romans 5:8, "But God demonstrates his own love for us in this: While we were still sinners, Christ died for us" (NIV).

Paul goes on to explain God's love for us in his letter to the Ephesian church: "In love he predestined us for adoption to himself as sons through Jesus Christ, according to the purpose of his will, to the praise of his glorious grace, with which he has blessed us in the Beloved" (Ephesians 1:4–6). What Paul is saying is that because God loved us and out of an overflow of his love, God foreknew and pre-called us for adoptions as sons. He chose you in love, before you were you, for the specific purpose of adopting you. This adoption is not one of obligation, convenience, or gain, but one of deep love and a desire to be in relationship with you. God did all this through Jesus. In other words, Jesus' sacrifice (death and resurrection) made it possible for God to pour out his love on you by adoption. This is a picture of a much-loved child drawn in, loved, and cared for by an incredibly loving Father.

There is still so much to say about this passage! It was God's will to adopt us in love; therefore, it was his will to sacrifice his beloved Son. Jesus' death was not unlucky happenstance but God's specific design. Why? Because the depths of God's grace, demonstrated in the ransom and redemption of sinful man through Jesus Christ, is now praised! This plan, this sacrifice, shows us the incredible, limitless depths of God's love and grace! As you repeatedly experience the ramifications of this blessing, how can you not be in awe of this kind of love, of this depth of grace, of this magnificent God, who is our Father?

In a letter to the early church, the apostle John describes God's love revealed through Jesus Christ as "real love—not that we loved God, but that he loved us and sent his Son as a sacrifice to take away our sins" (1 John 4:10). And he goes on to urge us to love one another because we have received such love: "Dear friends, since God loved us that much, we surely ought to love each other" (v. 11). This is why we must be loving toward others.

This passage is specifically talking about Christians loving other Christians; however, let me take this concept of loving others a step further. Let me argue that we should treat our co-workers, peers, and patients with such love, because the same Jesus and Lord who poured out his love for you, Christian, also poured out his love for your lost patient and your unbelieving friend.

Paul breaks it down for us by saying, "For the love of Christ controls us, because we have concluded this: that one has died for all, therefore all have died; and he died for all, that those who live might no longer live for themselves but for him who for their sake died and was raised." (2 Corinthians 5:14–15). This letter that Paul wrote the Corinthian church shows us that our love is unique. It is exceptional, because it is Christ's love at work in us, propelling us to the lost in love. Do you see? God is calling you to the unique work of his will. And it is his will to love and draw the lost to the world that they may be adopted as sons and daughters and ultimately experience the full and satisfying love of the Father.

This sounds great in theory, but in actuality, how does it play out? Honestly, is everyone jumping for joy because they love the Father? No, not even those of us who are privileged to live in a country where we are not persecuted for our faith. In 1 John 3, the apostle John confirms what we know to be true, that the world does hate us (v. 13), but we are still to love. Just because others hate Christ in us does not mean that we are off the hook from loving them. We are to love one another in spite of reciprocal hatred.

Why should we love in response to hatred? In 1 John 4:19, John says, "We love because he first loved us" (NIV). This was demonstrated when "the love of God was made manifest among us, that God sent his only Son into the world, so that we might live through him" (v. 4:9). Also, John tells us that it is impossible to love God and not love others, because "God is love" (v. 8). He then goes on to tell us that we are in actually commanded to love: "And this is his *commandment*, that we believe in the name of his Son Jesus Christ and love one another, just as he has commanded us" (3:23, author's emphasis). Lastly, John tells us that our love for others is the evidence of God's presence in our lives and his working in our hearts. He says, "Whoever keeps his commandments abides in God, and God in him. And by this we know that he abides in us, by the Spirit whom he has given us" (1 John 3:24).

Beloved, this world is evil and broken. It is filled with people who love evil and wickedness and hate anything that is of God, but he calls us deeper still. We are not bound by this world. Isn't it amazing that we serve a God who loves us? Let's live in that deep love, as we were created to. In turn his love will overflow from our hearts and into the lives of those around us.

I hope I am not belittling how difficult this is. It is a hard thing to love those who are hateful and hardhearted. However, Jesus sees your effort and toil and calls you to look past your circumstances. 1 Peter 3:14–16 says,

But even if you should suffer for righteousness' sake, you will be blessed. Have no fear of them, nor be troubled, but in your hearts, honor Christ the Lord as holy, always being prepared to make a defense to anyone who asks you for the reason for the hope that is in you; yet do it with gentleness and respect, having a good conscience, so that, when you are slandered, those who revile your good behavior in Christ may be put to shame.

Your work and your life is your ministry, through which God will reveal the light, abundant life, and hope that is found in him.

Let me give you a picture of what I mean. Recently the specialty team I work with was advertising its groundbreaking work in other countries. Due to the success of our team, using cutting-edge technology, infants with chronically low blood sugar, a fatal condition, were not only living but thriving. Many young patients now had the hope of being cured, and others had a protocol that would allow them to live long and healthy lives.

One family came to our hospital, hoping for a cure, from a country in the Middle East. The nurses on our floor provided exceptional care, and those who were Christians loved the family. The nurses were not often treated with kindness, but Christ's love shone brilliantly nonetheless. The family's hospital liaison mentioned that they had asked her why everyone was so happy. They couldn't wrap their minds around it. Sadly, she told them that it was just merely our culture to be friendly. When I heard this, my heart broke. Somewhere, we Christians had failed! We aren't kind, loving, or joyful merely because it is our culture; we are all these things because we live in the love of Christ, who has saved us and given us hope, a future, and purpose! Beloved, it is good to be loving, to let Christ's love overflow in your life. However, it should not end there! May we become a bold people who are ready and willing to shout from the rooftops the source of our love and joy.

Christ suffered and died so that he might reconcile the world to God. Therefore, we must approach difficulty and suffering with the same attitude, that we might, through God's grace overflowing in us, draw others to Christ. It is this perspective change, this mind shift, through which the Holy Spirit transforms us. When we move beyond living for our own comforts, desires, ambitions, and passions to living to be used by God, his will can be at work in our lives. And it is his will at work in us that impacts the lives of those around us.

Let me argue (as I believe Paul does in 2 Timothy 2) that suffering and difficulty are necessary and useful in bringing others to God. When we change our perspective of suffering and hardships, our hearts are reoriented to what is important, our first Love. This reorientation makes us dependent on God, and this dependence grows in us an ever-increasing desire to follow God's will, regardless of the hardship. Beloved, we will never fully seek God's will over our own without learning to suffer well, as Christ did. Therefore, since suffering and hardship are both inevitable and good for our soul, let us cling to Christ, our rock.

Let me jump in right here and cry out, DO NOT BE DISCOURAGED. God does not abandon us to our trials and difficulties and pain and suffering. God is ever-present, waiting for you to turn to him in your brokenness and in the darkness. Psalm 32:7 says, "You are a hiding place for me; you preserve me from trouble; you surround me with shouts of deliverance." Don't run and hide anywhere but in the arms of your God! He is a refuge. He will save you and keep you going. He will remind you and shout to you truth over the noise of the enemy. What will he remind you of? That he *will* deliver you.

Again, I am not trying to be cavalier about this subject. It is easy to type but incredibly difficult in practice. Joyfully enduring difficulty is contrary to our nature, and often in the depths of suffering all seems hopeless and the whole world dark. Even King David struggled to see God in the midst of his troubles. He said, "My tears have been my food day and night, while they say to me all the day long, 'Where is your God?' These things I remember as I pour out my soul . . . Why are you cast down, O my soul, and why are you in turmoil within me? Hope in God; for I shall again praise him, my salvation" (Psalm 42:3–5). David was bogged down with the hardship he was enduring, with the lies he was hearing, but he found hope and joy in the salvation that was surely coming.

Okay, let's be real. How do we make God our hiding place? How do we turn to him? By looking for him in his Word. This means consistently opening your Bible and reading it, even when you do not feel like it. Psalm 119:114 says, "You are my hiding place and my shield; I hope in your word." Dear friends, God's Word changes you. Look for God in his Word. Read it in desperation, looking for hope. Read it to draw closer to him. His Word is a life jacket that will keep your head above the towering waves in the stormy seas of life. And he will change you in those storms. You will find, as the storm subsides and the waves calm, that though you still come to God's Word hungry and desperate for more, it is no longer the storm that propels you to him but a deep love for his Word. Like King David, you will be changed to *love* God's commands and standards for living. God's Word will become your treasure and light. It will bring you hope and define your life as you grow in wisdom and in understanding.

This is how you become more wholly devoted to God, through the love of God's Word, through time spent reading and studying it. Then God will become your hiding place. How can you rest in God and fully trust him if you don't know his character? And how can you know his character unless you see him interact with various kinds of people (both good and bad) over a long period of time? How do you know if he is trustworthy unless you see him keep his Word? And how can you see all these things unless you open the Bible and read it? Too often we underestimate the power of God's Word. It is with his *spoken Word* that God created the world and the universe beyond! God's written Word is just as significant, authoritative, and powerful. It has the power to revive, restore, and save, and we see evidence of that throughout the narrative found in the Bible.

A Labor of Love

Now, having discussed Christ's calling to see past our situations, what does Jesus see? It sounds very philosophical to "see past your circumstances," but practically speaking, what are we trying to see? What is Jesus trying to get us to perceive that we may not yet be perceiving? Based on what we learned about God's will to reconcile the world back to himself, I would say that one of the first things Christ sees is the lost. Matthew 9:36 says, "When he saw the crowds, he had compassion for them, because they were harassed and helpless, like sheep without a shepherd." When Jesus looks out on our overpopulated world, he sees those who do not know him, those who have not been reconciled to the Father. They stand out to him in their helplessness and hopelessness. He is moved by their brokenness and oppression.

The book of Hosea shows us God's desire for the broken and oppressed. It reveals to us that God has more in store for us than such darkness. As I read through the book I am reminded of particular patients who lived in this dark brokenness on a daily basis—kids who were pimping themselves out for drugs. God called and gave hope to several prostitutes in the Bible, including Gomer of Hosea's story. God sees the abuse, the injustice, and the damaged soul. No one is too far gone, and the prostitutes included in the Bible are proof of that. If the Lord called them and changed their lives and hearts, he can do the same for us. This is hope for the lost, for the battered and oppressed! Jesus Christ, the Beloved, can and will restore, bring peace and safety! Open your eyes and see that Jesus is calling the lost, longing to fill the gaps in their souls with his light, life, and love.

So, after Jesus sees the lost in Matthew 9, he zooms out, so to speak, to the bigger picture. "Then he said to his disciples, 'The harvest is plentiful, but the laborers are few; therefore pray earnestly to the Lord of the harvest to send out laborers into his harvest'" (v. 37). Let me break this down. Jesus looked out over the crowds and saw brokenness, oppression, and great need. And then he started talking about a harvest. It seems like a jump, but it's really a vantage point change. He was trying to get his disciples to understand that there was something bigger going on than broken people following him en masse.

This reference to a metaphorical harvest is to spark understanding. Jesus again uses this concept in John 4, when he says, "Look, I tell you, lift up your eyes, and see that the fields are white for harvest. Already the one who reaps is receiving wages and gathering fruit for eternal life, so that the sower and reaper may rejoice together . . . I sent you to reap that for which you did not labor. Others have labored, and you have entered into their labor" (vv. 35–36, 38). This gives us a better understanding of what Jesus was trying to communicate. God doesn't merely see lost and broken souls but is at work gathering those lost souls for eternity to come. And this process of gathering souls is accomplished through your faithful work, beloved.

God's desire is for all of mankind to be in a right relationship with him, and he will use you to accomplish this purpose. However, we also learn from the Matthew and John passages that the work is hard and it's a work that few are willing to partake in. Jesus says, "pray earnestly to the Lord of the harvest to send out laborers into his harvest." The ratio that is presented to us not equal. There is a sense that there is an impossibly large number of people who are ready to be drawn to the Father but very few who have the drive and ability to show them the way to reconciliation.

However hard and seemingly endless the work may be, in these passages we also we see God's mercy and goodness to his faithful workers. First off, God pays what the worker has earned. This is not a "prosperity gospel" that I'm talking about but spiritual treasures that are waiting for the faithful, hardworking believer in eternity to come. And in addition to earning wages, we are "gathering fruit for eternal life." This means that we get to experience God's work firsthand. He has invited us to use our hands and experience the results of his movement. This is a treasure, though we may not recognize it yet. These two things reveal so much to us about God's character: he is right and just, rightly compensating the worker for his faithful labor, and he is generous, giving the laborer the joys experiencing of his handiwork as he labors. Therefore, the worker is given much, both in the present and in eternity. God has not called you to a thankless toil, but a joyful work that will cause you to experience him personally and undeniably while being grown and strengthened in the labor.

Finally, in these passages, we see that as we enter into this harvest work, we are stepping into the legacy of our spiritual predecessors. Jesus tells us, "I sent you to reap that for which you did not labor. Others have labored, and you have entered into their labor." Let me say this to you, as gently as I can. You cannot "break" the harvest. Nor are you likely to see the whole work from start to finish. God is the "Lord of the harvest." He designates assignments and determines work times. However, we can know this with certainty: the work will be completed, whether by your hand or by another's. We do not determine the harvest; we are here to work and are invited to watch the miraculous saving of the multitudes!

Kingdom Work

But to what end do we toil and labor? What is the purpose of drawing people to the Lord beyond their reconciliation to him? This is all kingdom work, which is a very "churchy" way of saying that this work is for the establishment of God's kingdom here on earth. It's a concept that is hard to imagine, because at this point in history we are talking in spiritual terms, with the hope of a future physical reality. Jesus, understanding the limits of our human ability to comprehend something that is invisible to us, describes the kingdom of God in Matthew 13 using a handful of pictures.

The first picture he gives us is in verses 24–30. It's a picture story of a sower who plans for and plants good, fruitful seed. His enemy attempts to sabotage his good efforts by planting weeds throughout the field. Rather than risk the wellbeing of the good crop, the sower waits until the plant is mature and is bearing fruit (wheat) before pulling the fruitless, useless weeds and burning them. Then he turns back to his harvest, which is now as he intended, and brings it into his barn.

From this story we see that the kingdom of God is made up of people who are intentionally prepared for bearing fruit. They are important to God and are not considered expendable. Their time of growth and maturing is on earth, in the soil, but their purpose will be realized after God gathers his people. During their time of growth, they may be surrounded by people whose only purpose is to thwart God's plan. However, regardless of the intent of the weeds or the enemy, the harvest still happens. God's people are still gathered; God's plan still happens. Thus, God's kingdom is still fully established, though the enemy may try to prevent it from happening.

The second picture he paints is of a mustard seed. He says, "The kingdom of heaven is like a grain of mustard seed that a man took and sowed in his field. It is the smallest of all seeds, but when it has grown it is larger than all the garden plants and becomes a tree, so that the birds of the air come and make nests in its branches" (vv. 31–32). We are shown that God's kingdom starts small, with one seed, and grows beyond all expectations into something huge. So huge that it is inviting to others who are not even a part of it. They want to be near it. God's kingdom is attractive and beneficial to all, even those who chase after the wind.

Immediately following this illustration, to describe the effect of the kingdom of God on the world, Jesus paints a picture of a woman adding yeast to flour to make bread (v. 33). It only takes a few granules of yeast compared to the three measures of flour needed, but those few small granules have a profound effect on the flour. With or without the yeast, bread can be made, but the quality of the bread significantly increases with the yeast. Therefore, Jesus is saying that the kingdom of God may be made up of far fewer people than the world outside, but the few have far more impact than those who are not a part of the kingdom. In fact, they influence the world and elevate others beyond their own capacity.

From these two stories we see that Jesus is trying to get us to understand that his kingdom has a significant and lasting impact on the world, for good. That though Jesus may have seemed insignificant, he established a kingdom that is unmoving and inviting, that impacts even those who are not a part of the kingdom, for their good and growth.

Next Jesus describes how valuable the kingdom is. He says, "The kingdom of heaven is like a treasure hidden in a field, which a man found and covered up. Then in his joy he goes and sells all that he has and buys that field. Again, the kingdom of heaven is like a merchant in search of fine pearls, who, on finding one pearl of great value, went and sold all he had and bought it" (vv. 45–46). In this passage there are two kinds of people described: those who stumble across the kingdom and those who are looking for the kingdom. In both cases, their response is the same. They recognize the value of what they found and sell all they own to keep this treasure.

This shows us that there are those who stumble across Jesus. They are not looking for him but quickly recognize that he is the "real deal" when they find him. Then there are those who are looking for meaning and fulfillment in life. They are looking for what is real and finally find it, in Jesus. Both men in Jesus' stories are filled with joy and satisfaction because they found something that was more valuable than the sum of what they had. The kingdom of God, which is found only through Jesus, is of more value than the sum of all you have, even if you are the richest person on earth.

Jesus then gives his final illustration: "The kingdom of God is like a net that was thrown into the sea and gathered fish of every kind. When it was full, men drew it ashore and sat down and sorted the good into containers but threw away the bad" (vv. 47–48). God draws all kinds of people to himself, yet in masses of fish there are those who are "good" and those who are "bad." It is not until the fish are individually inspected that they can be known as either good or bad, righteous or wicked.

All of these parables have a common theme. God is drawing people to himself, and there are two classifications of people. There are those who are usable and those who are useless. And it is their righteousness, or conversely their wickedness, that determines how useful or useless they are. This is hard to hear. It is difficult to hear that there are people who have no place in God's kingdom. It is painful to think that not everyone who is drawn to God or planted in God's field will be a part of the kingdom that they benefit from. Do you feel the heaviness? I do. And I have a difficult time typing these truths.

You see, God's kingdom is about more than the masses. God's kingdom is about his creation that follows him. It is always about the heart—those deep motives that shape who we are. God's kingdom is like a beautiful musical composition. He is the melody and creation is the harmony. God calls everyone to join in the chorus, but not everyone wants to sing along. Some people want to sing their own song, even though it clashes with the music surrounding them. Why would God include them and make a place for them in his choir if they refuse to sing his song? What else is there to do but reject those who are so stubborn in their refusal to join the harmonies of creation?

Let me give you another picture to work with. In Jeremiah 24, God shows the prophet Jeremiah two baskets. One is filled with good, newly ripened figs. The other basket is filled with very bad, rotting figs. The first basket represents the people who were captured and exiled to Babylon. These people were good fruit, righteous, usable by God, and so he would continue to work his sovereign plan through them. They would experience restoration, growth, renewal, and fulfillment of promise. Though they still had to bear the consequences of their actions and the actions of the previous generations, God would be with them, for them, and at work within them.

The second basket represents those who were either left behind or scattered to other countries. They were wicked and rotten people who would have no part in God's plan. Their punishment would be harsh. They would be cut off from the promises made to their forefathers and would never be "at home," no matter where they went. They would be looked on with disgust, contempt, and disapproval.

In this prophesy we again see this seemingly harsh and difficult sorting of the righteous and unrighteous, the useful and unusable. But then, just in case we have forgotten, just a few verses later in Jeremiah 25:3, God reminds us that this seemingly callous treatment of Israel is the result of years of ignoring the Lord and the call to wholly follow him. Genesis 26:4 tells us that it was always God's intention to fully bless Israel (the descendants of Abraham) and all the nations of the world. God's intention has always been to draw everyone to himself, but sin makes everything bitter.

Beloved, our hearts should be heavy for the kingdom of God. We should be burdened by the lost, by the multitudes who do not know our good Father. The harvest is abundant, and God's kingdom is coming. The multitudes are being gathered, and you are being called to participate in eternity.

Let me end with what the kingdom of heaven is. Once we move past the bitterness that sin brings to the story, we learn that God's kingdom is a beautiful, harmonious mingling of God's people. It is filled with the pursuit of holiness and deeper understanding of the Lord. It is rich community without sin tainting our relationships and interactions. It is people fully living in God's power while his power is displayed in their daily lives. And in everything from the big to the minute, God is praised and glorified.[2]

The even deeper beauty is that this beautiful future is not only reserved for Israel, but for all the nations, for those who are "partakers of the promise in Christ Jesus through the gospel" (Ephesians 3:6). Titus 2:11–14 tells us,

> For the grace of God has appeared, bringing salvation for all people, training us to renounce ungodliness and worldly passions, and to live self-controlled, upright, and godly lives in the present age, waiting for our blessed hope, the appearing of the glory of our great God and Savior Jesus Christ, who gave himself for us to redeem us from all lawlessness and to purify for himself a people for his own possession who are zealous for good works.

This is why we work. This is why God called us to care for the sick. For the purpose of drawing people to God, that they might taste and see that he is good. That they might come to know the hope and life waiting for them. That by one life at a time, creation might be reconciled to her Maker in joy and abundant life. Today, pray for your peers, that they might be saved. And ask your savior for boldness to proclaim the good news of salvation that comes through Christ Jesus!

---

[2] Acts 2:42–47

10

The Kingdom of God

I have this picture in my mind. I look out over a vast plain at sunset. The entire plain is filled with wheat that is ready for the harvest. The soft gold tones contrast with a deepening red sky. Night is rapidly approaching, and there is an impossible amount of work to be done. A soft breeze touches my cheek as I watch the wheat dance in its caress. I look past the sea of yellow to the mountains looming in the distance. Soon. Soon the mountains will be upon us. Soon I will climb their peaks, but for now, it is time to work. I take a breath to settle my restless heart and look, once again, over the vast expanse of harvest before me. Such bittersweet emotions. In eagerness I recognize there is so much to accomplish, and in sadness I see that there are too few working. Night is almost upon us and there are still multitudes that have yet to receive Christ. If only there were more brothers and sisters who would partake in the grueling and joyful work before me.

This image is one that haunts me. It is one that reminds me of what is real and gives me hope for the future. Daily I struggle to see beyond my own temporary circumstances. I am often too quickly bogged down by the logistics that make my profession functional. In those moments and days, I take my eyes off my goal and focus instead on the waves threatening to crest over my head. Then God uses that beautiful, haunting picture to remind me to look up and see beyond the temporary, to see the world with kingdom eyes.

In the last few chapters, we have talked about our calling as defenders of God's glory. We learned that there is an unseen spiritual battle waging around us and we are expected to engage. Together we looked at the tools that God has given us to aid our fight against the enemy. And most importantly, we learned who the enemy is in light of the Almighty God, our God. Now, I want to tell you that resisting the enemy is only part of our calling. The other part is working.

Matthew 5:9 says, "Blessed are the peacemakers, for they shall be called sons of God." Though we are to defiantly resist Satan and the work of the enemy, we are to be peacemakers. Remember that our battle is not against flesh and blood. Our battle is not against humanity. It is against sin, the prince of darkness and his foes. By contrast, we are to love those around us. This is a love that births peace and testifies of the one to whom we belong. As we make peace with our friends and families, co-workers and patients, they will look at our loving actions of peace and think, "That is a Christian, a son of God."

Jesus then lovingly tells us our purpose in our work. He says, "You are the salt of the earth" (v. 13) and "You are the light of the world" (v. 14). God has given us and positioned us for the task of being a preservative to the decaying world and light in the darkness. Everything about us, our whole purpose and character, is a reflection of Christ, of God's work in the world. Are you following me? God has crafted you for the specific purpose of being so inherently Christlike that you shine like a beacon. And in his grace, your radiance that sets you apart as unique is also the force that allows you to have firsthand experience of his redemptive work in the world.

People want more salt, and people crave the light. They are drawn to the little reflections of their Creator, and God has allowed you to be that beacon that draws people to salvation! Isn't that so incredible? God is giving you a front row seat to his awesome power and incredible plan! However, this front row seat comes with a price. And that price is your time and effort.

Jesus tells his disciples, "The harvest is plentiful, but the laborers are few; therefore pray earnestly to the Lord of the harvest to send out more laborers into his harvest" (Matthew 9:37 – 38). It is interesting that the call of the harvest is placed after a story of redemption, of Jesus' bringing someone from hopeless darkness to light. I believe this is the intentional inspiration of the Holy Spirit, because Jesus is calling his followers to labor with him in rescuing people. He is calling us to toil with him as he breaks their chains and pulls them from the jaws of spiritual death.

Did you pick up on the last part of the verse? He says that compared to the number of people who are hungry and ready for hope in Christ Jesus, there are so few people who are willing to partake in the hard work of drawing them to Christ. Beloved, are you willing to work? Are you willing to sacrifice your time, pour out your heart, and struggle to pull people to life? There is still time, but it is running short. We do not know when our Savior will return, but it, God willing, will be sooner than we expect.

Practically, what does it look like to work for the kingdom of God? In Romans 10, Paul says, "everyone who calls on the name of the Lord will be saved" (v. 13), and he raises a question: "How then will they call on him whom they have not believed?" (v. 14). Paul recognizes that you have to believe in a person, trust their ability and character, to call to them for help. But, he continues, "how are they to believe in him of whom they have never heard?" That is, how can someone possibly believe in God if they have never even heard of God? Lastly he asks, "And how are they to hear without someone preaching?" Paul is arguing that there can be no knowledge of God without someone teaching others about God. This is not solely pulpit preaching that Paul is talking about, but a passing on of the knowledge of God, even from caregivers to patients. However, passing on of the knowledge of God can only happen when someone is sent, much like a messenger. The message will never get passed on unless the messenger is sent.

Paul then points the reader to Isaiah 52:7, saying, "How beautiful are the feet of those who preach the good news!" (v. 15). The actual text in Isaiah is a little different. It says, "How beautiful upon the mountains are the feet of him who brings good news, who publishes peace, who brings good news of happiness, who publishes salvation, who says to Zion, 'Your God reigns.'" You cannot help but get the sense that the journey to deliver the message is long, difficult, and so very incredible. Travelling through the mountains is tiring and hard on the body, especially on the feet. After miles of climbing, working your way around boulders, your feet would be dusty and likely tired, if not sore. Yet, God says those dusty, tired things are *beautiful*. Beloved, your obedience is beautiful to your King.

This begs the question, why? Why does God consider your toil and effort to be beautiful? Because you are bringing the good news of reconciliation to people who have no hope of reconciliation, to those who do not even know that there is good news to be found. My friends, this is not just any good news. This is the good news of salvation through Jesus Christ. It is a message of peace, of hope, and it brings lasting joy to all who will hear, believe, and respond by crying out to God for salvation.

Brothers and sisters, from the times of old, since the fall of man, it has been God's intention that everyone. Every. Single. Person. Be saved and reconciled back to God. This is the heartbeat of God's kingdom, that all of creation would come back to her Creator and be fully satisfied in him. *Everyone* who calls on his name will be saved. This anthem is echoed through the generations and declared by the prophet Joel[1] in the Old Testament and the apostle Paul in the New Testament, as we have already seen. So there is no room for misunderstanding, Paul proclaims, "For there is no distinction between Jew and Greek; for the same Lord is Lord of all, bestowing his riches on all who call on him" (Romans 10:12). Thus, our hope is not reserved for a choice, lucky few, but is available to anyone who would cry out to God.

Beloved we must cry out in boldness! We must shout out this hope with confidence! Jesus gives us the green light to declare the gospel with reckless abandon when he says, "The time is fulfilled, and the kingdom of God is at hand" (Mark 1:15). There is no other time but now. God's kingdom is here; the time for action is now. Do you feel the urgency?

Right before his ascension into heaven, Jesus told his disciples, "All authority in heaven and on earth has been given to me. Go therefore and make disciples of all nations, baptizing them in the name of the Father and of the Son and of the Holy Spirit, teaching them to observe all that I have commanded you" (Matthew 28:18–20). These verses reveal to us that Jesus operates under the full authority of the Father, so his command to share the good news of salvation was fully within his right as sovereign. In fact, because Jesus has been given all of the Father's authority, the heartbeat of the Father is the heartbeat of the Son, and he is now making it our heartbeat as well. Reconciliation of the lost to the Father must be our passion, as much as it is our duty, because we are little reflectors of the Almighty.

The story of John the Baptist is such a foreshadowing of our own calling. John the Baptist was called by God to "prepare the way of the Lord" (Mark 1:3). We, in turn, are called to share the gospel to all people. John is described as "a voice . . . calling in the wilderness." We are likewise to be voices calling out in a spiritual wilderness. John's

---

[1] Joel 2:32

purpose was to call attention to Jesus, the fact that salvation had indeed come. His mission was to point people to salvation. And this too is our purpose and mission.

Toward the end of John chapter 1, we see Jesus call his disciples. These were men who were looking for the Messiah. They were hungry, hopeful, and then, BAM, they met Jesus. They came face-to-face with the fulfillment of their longing and searching. Beloved, your patients, peers, family, and friends are hungry for more. Whether they say so or not, they are longing and looking for Christ. However, as one commentary puts it, "People in sin are in such darkness that they need someone to tell them what is light."[2]

John states, "The light shines in the darkness, and the darkness has not overcome it . . . to all who did receive him, who believed in his name, he gave the right to become children of God" (John 1:5, 12). It does not matter what darkness God leads you through to save the hopeless, the light shines in the darkness and the light of Christ will always conquer. The light is dawning and the hopeless darkness is being chased away.

I want so desperately for you to understand that this work, though hard, is work that you can complete in victory, confidence, and joy. As sons and daughters redeemed by the blood of the Lamb, we have been called to action, to partake in Christ's ministry of reconciliation. His work on earth has now become ours. The prophet Isaiah spoke of this kingdom work, for which Jesus condescended to come:

> The Spirit of the LORD GOD is upon me,
> because the LORD has anointed me
> to bring good news to the poor;
> he has sent me to bind up the brokenhearted,
> to proclaim liberty to the captives,
> and the opening of the prison to those who are bound;
> to proclaim the year of the LORD's favor.

Jesus' ministry while on earth was characterized by restoration, hope, compassion, rejoicing and reconciliation to God. It marked the beginning of spiritual prosperity for those who follow him. The Great

---

[2] Louis A. Barbieri, et al., The Bible Knowledge Commentary: New Testament (1983).

Commission of Matthew 28 is a calling to this ministry in the power and strength of the Holy Spirit.

Beloved, this is why God called you and specifically placed you in your career at this time. You are to be used powerfully by God to proclaim hope, to heal, to restore, and to rejoice. Brothers and Sisters, *this is the year of the Lord's favor* because salvation has come! *This is the year of the Lord's favor* because Christ has poured out the Holy Spirit on us to continue his ministry. Salvation is still at hand for those who do not know Christ, and it is still the year of the Lord's favor because Jesus has not yet returned and God's final judgment has not yet come.

What a beautiful time to be alive and following Jesus! Not only has Christ poured out his Spirit to save mankind, we know from Matthew 9 that hearts are ready and hungry to know Jesus. They are desperate to be saved. Therefore, we can step with confidence into our careers, because Christ has set this ministry before us.

What a journey this has been. I hope the Lord has changed you as much as he has transformed me through it. My hope and prayer is that through His Word, God will breathe new life into your work. Your efforts are seen, and your toil will be rewarded. More than that, your faithful service to the Lord, in whatever capacity he has called you, is making eternal impact. You might not be parting the Red Sea, but your faithful reflection of Christ and bold declaration of the gospel is infinitely more powerful. And the fruit of your labor is proof of God's power at work in you. Praise the Lord! Salvation has come, and the Almighty has invited you to follow him into the heartbeat of his kingdom. God has so much more for us than we could imagine. If we only had the eyes to see.

Bibliography

Baker, Walter L., Craig Blasising, J. Ronald Blue, Sid S. Buzzell, and Donald K. Campbell. *The Bible Knowledge Commentary: Old Testament*, ed. John F. Walvoord (Colorado Springs: Cook Communications Minitries, 1983).

Barbieri, Louis A., J. Ronald Blue, Edwin A. Blum, Donald K. Campbell, and Thomas L. Constable, *The Bible Knowledge Commentary: New Testament*, ed. John F. Walvoord and Roy B. Zuck (Colorado Springs: Cook Communications Ministries, 1983).

Chandler, Matt, "The Power of Song," *TVC Resources*, https://www.tvcresources.net/resource-library/sermons/the-power-of-song, (The Village Church, 2018).

Evans, Tony, *The Battle is the Lord's* (Chicago: Moody Press, 1998).

Henry, Matthew. *The Matthew Henry Commentary: The Classic Work with Updated Language*, ed. Martin H. Manser (Grand Rapids: Zondervan, 2010).

Keller, Timothy, "Sin as Predator," *Gospel In Life*, https://gospelinlife.com/downloads/sin-as-predator-6427/, (1996).

Merriam-Webster, inc., https://www.merriam-webster.com/dictionary.

Neale, Micheal and Krissy Nordhoff, "Your Great Name" (2011).

Pink, Arthur W, *The Attributes of God*. (Grand Rapids: Baker Books, 2006).

Piper, John, "The Meanings of Love in the Bible," https://www.desiringgod.org/articles/the-meanings-of-love-in-the-bible, (Desiring God, 1975).

Piper, John, "What is Sin? The Essence and Root of All Sinning," https://www.desiringgod.org/messages/the-origin-essence-and-definition-of-sin, (Desiring God, 2015).

Rend Collective, "Weep With Me," *Good News* (2018).

The Oh Hellos, "Eat You Alive," *Through the Deep, Dark Valley* (2012).

Acknowledgements

Writing this book has been such a refining adventure and would have been impossible without the help and support of the following people.

I first and foremost want to acknowledge and thank my husband. His support, encouragement, and help have been not only invaluable, but the fuel for this project. I cannot sing enough praises for this man who took on the extra slack of parenting and cleaning over the past two and a half years. It is because of this incredible man- his wisdom, servant's heart and belief in this work that God has been in the midst of- that I have been able to carry this work to completion. Pico, thank you for all the million things you have done, the encouragement when I doubted myself and wanted to give up, and for your Godly wisdom that you guided me with. I love you even more today, because your character has shown through in deeper ways during the course of this journey.

I would also like to thank my friends and family who have encouraged me over the past couple of years. I am so grateful for those of you who read my manuscript, especially when it was in its rough draft! Thank you for your feedback, your endorsements, your kind words, and your support to continue this good work. You have given me confidence in God's work and the courage to continue writing. Thank you.

To my editor, Brittany Clarke, thank you for your hard work and insights into my writing. Without your expertise, this work would be a hot mess. Thank you.

To my sister-in-law and killer cover designer, thank you. What a gift you have given me through your incredible artistic abilities. Your hard work and thoughtful creativity has given this book a beautiful face that will, God willing, grace many bookshelves! Thank you a million times over!

And most importantly, I must acknowledge and thank my Creator. He used this research, this journey and his word to soothe my aching heart and answer the deep questions I had been wrestling with. His timing, plans, and calling are perfect. Never would I have imagined I would write a book, and yet in His mercy he gave me this book to write, so that my own heart might be changed. He is indeed a Good Shepherd who cares for the hearts of his children. All glory be to his beautiful name!

About the Author

Sara Hill is a wife, mother, nurse, author and Jesus follower. When she is not practicing her alligator wrestling skills by wrangling her three children, she can be found working in one the best children's hospitals in the nation. With almost a decade of bedside nursing under her belt, she has spent thousands of hours and steps loving on children and striving to shine the light of the gospel in her practice. For more information on the author or her other projects, please visit her website at www.saradaniellehill.com

1

$$f(x) = -5x - 7$$

$$y = -5x - 7$$

$$x = -5y - 7$$

$$y = -\frac{x}{5} - \frac{7}{5}$$

$$f(x) = -5x - 7$$

$$f^{-1}(x = -\frac{x}{5} - \frac{7}{5}$$

2) $3 - x \geq 0$

$x \leq 3$

$1 - x \geq 0$

$x \leq 1$

$\sqrt{1-x} = 0$

$x = 1$

$(-\infty, 1)$